PENGUIN ENTERPRISE

INSPIRED

Gnanvatsaldas Swami, D.Litt., is a distinguished Life Coach and Eminent Speaker from the Bochasanwasi Akshar Purushottam Swaminarayan Sanstha (BAPS). After graduating as a mechanical engineer from BVM College of Engineering, Gujarat, India, he embarked on a spiritual journey under the guidance of His Holiness Pramukh Swami Maharaj, former leader of BAPS and the sixth spiritual successor of Bhagwan Swaminarayan.

Gnanvatsaldas Swami's magnetic presence and eloquent oratory have sparked positive transformations worldwide, captivating audiences across various platforms, from social media to prestigious universities and corporate events. As a prolific columnist, his weekly articles in leading newspapers command a vast readership.

With over three decades of experience and more than 15,500 life-enhancement talks delivered, Gnanvatsaldas Swami's influence extends beyond borders, having interacted with millions in over 32 countries. His commitment to social service is evident in over 24,700 home visits, where he has provided families with spiritual guidance and practical support. Recognized for his dedication, he has received two honorary Doctor of Literature degrees, the prestigious 'Suryaratna—The Saint of Modern India' award and official citations from the New York State Assembly and other US cities.

As an ambassador of universal harmony, Gnanvatsaldas Swami tirelessly travels, fulfilling his guru's vision of reaching out to every individual seeking a better quality of life.

inspired

DAILY WISDOM *for* HOLISTIC LIVING

GNANVATSALDAS SWAMI

PENGUIN
ENTERPRISE

An imprint of Penguin Random House

PENGUIN ENTERPRISE

Penguin Enterprise is an imprint of the Penguin Random House group of companies whose addresses can be found at global.penguinrandomhouse.com

Published by Penguin Random House India Pvt. Ltd
4th Floor, Capital Tower 1, MG Road,
Gurugram 122 002, Haryana, India

First published in Penguin Enterprise by Penguin Random House India 2025

ISBN 9780143473763

Typeset in Bembo Std
Printed at Replika Press Pvt. Ltd, India

www.penguin.co.in

To my guru, Mahant Swami Maharaj,
and to all who believe in the potential for positive change.

CONTENTS

Foreword   xi

Preface   xiii

Introduction   xix

SECTION 1: PERSONAL GROWTH

8+8+8   3

Healthy, Wealthy, and Wise   8

Infinite Scroll   14

The Stress Solution   20

The Age of Distraction   28

Masks We Wear   34

The Endless Pursuit   37

Attitude is Everything   41

Seize the Day   48

Smoke and Ashes   52

Architects of Destiny   60

SECTION 2: FAMILY VALUES

Calm in the Chaos   69

'Why Should I?'   75

The Smouldering Log   81

War of Words   88

Quality Family Time   96

Project Sync   105

What Mark Will You Leave?   112

The Generation Gap   120

Parenting in the Digital World   125

Age of Honour   132

SECTION 3: WORK ETHICS
AND HUMAN RELATIONS

Values Stronger than Steel   143

The Wriggling Butterfly   152

Test of the Titans   159

The Path to Greatness   165

Work-Life Harmony   170

You're on Mute   177

Putting People First   183

Sweat of the Brow   190

The Dishwashing President   197

Be Big-Minded   204

SECTION 4: SPIRITUALITY

Just–in–Time Wisdom   215

Daily Reflection   222

What Can I Give?   228

Live Each Day as If It Were Your Last   234

Balanced Within   240

Beyond the Body   245

Cosmic Conversation   254

Seva   262

A Lotus in the Desert   270

The Role of Gurus   277

Acknowledgements   285

FOREWORD

3 October 2024
Junagadh, India

Pujya Gnanvatsal Swami,
Jai Shri Swaminarayan.

I have received the wonderful news of your recent completion of the book titled, *inspired: Daily Wisdom for Holistic Living*. My heartfelt congratulations to you on this remarkable achievement.

Your hard work, dedication, and sincere efforts in creating this valuable book are truly commendable. You have tirelessly used your wisdom to help countless individuals, and through this book, you will continue to impact many more. The four pillars of the book—Personal Growth, Family Values, Work Ethics & Human Relations, and Spirituality—are essential components for a well-rounded and fulfilling life. In today's world, with the rapid rise of technology and the fast-paced work and personal environments, there is an even greater need for individuals to take time for personal reflection and strive for balance in life.

Your book provides much-needed guidance in this regard, helping individuals develop their inner selves while maintaining strong relationships, ethics, and spiritual connection.

I am praying to Akshar-Purushottam Maharaj and Guruhari Pramukh Swami Maharaj that the readers of this book benefit deeply from its wisdom. May they imbibe the teachings and become well-rounded individuals rooted in moral and spiritual values, capable of thriving in all areas of their lives.

May Maharaj and Swami continue to bless you with strength and inspiration in your continued efforts to help others and may those who read this book apply its principles within their lives.

With blessings and prayers,

May all get great inspiration from this book.
Sadhu Keshavjivandas.

Jai Swaminarayan from Sadhu Keshavjivandas
HH Mahant Swami Maharaj
(Spiritual Head, BAPS Swaminarayan Sanstha)

PREFACE

1 April 1990, 12.01 a.m.

The dim glow of the moon cast long shadows over the APC student hostel, creating an eerie stillness perfect for our prank. As planned, our team of eight gathered in the corridor, each armed with flashlights and a shared sense of mischief.

'Everyone ready?' I whispered, receiving nods in response. We moved stealthily to the first dormitory. My friend carefully unscrewed the wall clock, another tiptoed over to the nightstand to pick up the alarm clock, and I gently lifted a wristwatch lying beside a sleeping student. We moved in silent choreography, listening carefully to the rhythmic snoring of our fellow students. Then, with synchronized precision, we set each clock three hours ahead. With a silent nod, we placed everything back exactly as it was.

'Next room,' I mouthed, and we silently slipped into the hallway.

'The door's locked,' my friend gestured, pointing towards the balcony. 'We'll have to climb over.'

One by one, we darted to the back and jumped catlike onto the neighbouring balcony, trying not to disturb the plants. 'Same routine,' I instructed. 'Just don't knock anything over.'

For the next few hours, we moved through the hostel, altering the time on every clock we could find. At 2.57 a.m., we regrouped near the central alarm system.

'Ready to change the bell time?' I asked my friend, who was already fiddling with the controls.

'I think I've got it,' he grinned, giving the thumbs up. 'DONG! DONG!'

'Quick! Scatter!' I ordered, and we all hurried to our hiding spots.

From behind the bushes, I watched in suppressed laughter as the 400 students groggily emerged from their rooms in their nightwear, rubbing their eyes and looking disorientated.

'What time is it?' one student asked, peering up at the dark sky with a puzzled expression.

'6 a.m.,' another said, staring at his watch with a frown.

'Then why do I feel so tired?'

As the crowd grew, their confusion turned to mild irritation. The students shuffled towards the main hall, grumbling about the early hour. Just as they started to sing the morning prayers, the rector appeared, looking equally perplexed.

'What's going on here?' he demanded, checking his pocket watch.

'Good morning, Sir,' a sleepy student replied. 'It's 6 a.m., isn't it?'

The rector's face twisted in confusion, then realization. 'It's 3 a.m.!' he bellowed, glaring around as the truth dawned on everyone. 'April Fools!' he added with a chuckle, realizing the prank.

The hall erupted in laughter, with students and seniors alike shaking their heads at the clever trick. As we joined the group, blending in with the amused crowd, my friend leaned over and whispered, 'Next year, we set the clocks back instead.'

'Deal,' I replied, grinning.

* * *

During my years studying engineering in Vallabh Vidyanagar, the educational hub of Gujarat, I frequently found myself testing the boundaries. Curfews and rules felt more like challenges than restrictions. Words like 'don't' and 'can't' only ignited my curiosity, making me ponder, 'What if?' and 'Why not?' My friends and I often broke curfew, scaled hostel walls, roamed the streets late at night, played impromptu cricket matches, and watched the latest movies. We thrived on adventure, returning in the early hours with nights full of unforgettable memories.

The APC hostel buzzed with youthful energy and activities. Every year, students showcased their talents on the annual day through dances, dramas, and art. In 1988, we were informed that Pramukh Swami Maharaj would visit our hostel. Though I barely knew him, I was scheduled to perform in his presence that year. I played the role of Dr Vangiya in a drama. I didn't see Swamiji again until ten months later in 1989, when I performed once more, this time as a jinn (spirit). Both times, I was heavily disguised with a beard, face paint, fake eyebrows, and detailed props. Swamiji didn't know me by name, and we hadn't spoken before. But after my performance, I approached him for his blessings. He briefly grasped my hands, looked directly into my eyes, and said with a smile, 'From Vangiya to Jinn.'

This moment struck me deeply. He had seen me twice on different occasions in very different costumes, yet he recognized me. When our eyes met, I was mesmerized by his deep brown eyes, filled with compassion and wisdom. He saw past my facades and into my heart. Despite being a common student among many, I felt he truly knew me. He saw my past, present, and future—even my flaws and limitations. Yet he accepted me wholly and unconditionally. He saw potential in me that I didn't know existed. 'This is someone extraordinary,' I thought to myself.

Thereafter, whenever Pramukh Swami Maharaj visited the APC hostel, I carefully observed his lifestyle and how he gave time for others. Among the crowds and in moments of solitude, I consistently saw his genuine, unassuming nature. He was dedicated, pure, and at peace. His presence had a calming effect on me. Once again, I asked myself, 'What if?' and 'Why not?' But this time, it was different. 'What if I could live a pure and decent life like Swamiji?' I considered. 'Why not dedicate myself to serving society?' I wondered. Over time, these thoughts matured and empowered me. Slowly but surely, my life took a new direction. I became disciplined, purposeful, and dedicated. I was truly inspired.

INTRODUCTION

23 May 1996, 8.50 a.m.

I lay sprawled helplessly on the highway, feeling both numbness and searing pain. My ears were ringing, and darkness engulfed me. Then there was a blinding light and a distorted voice. I closed my eyes, and a memory briefly flashed before me: the inside of a car, a passing traffic light, and then a bang. A sudden impact flung me out of the door, and now here I was, my body limp. I opened my eyes and saw a policeman, holding up a blurry hand. I saw four fingers, eight, twelve, and then four again. Then everything went blank. I felt my body rising into the air, the whirring of a helicopter, and then darkness.

More than 30 hours later, I woke up in a hospital bed. My right leg and arm were in a cast, wires were attached to my chest, and my head felt heavy. A friendly American doctor soon approached me to update me on what had happened. 'You're lucky to be alive,' he said. 'The car accident was terrible. But you're a swami, so you must be protected by God.'

He took out a photo and showed me the wrecked car. 'You were airlifted here to Atlantic City General Hospital. You've been passing in and out of consciousness, but scans show you are fine. There are four fractures in your right leg and two in your arm. Just take your time and get some rest.'

'Did I come here alone?' I asked.

'The driver and the other swami had only minor injuries,' he replied. 'So they were taken to a different hospital. The paramedic told me they wanted to join you in the air ambulance, but it's restricted to emergency patients.'

After giving my details, I was soon joined by Yagnavallabh Swami. He limped into the ward with a cast on his foot. 'Pramukh Swami Maharaj has been phoning from India every hour since the accident,' he said. 'He has been worried because we couldn't locate you.'

I was handed the phone and heard a familiar voice. 'Is this Gnanvatsal? How are you feeling? Are you okay?' Pramukh Swami Maharaj quickly asked.

'Yes, it's me. I am fine,' I answered, as my eyes filled with tears.

'Listen, your lifespan had come to an end,' Swamiji revealed. 'But due to God's grace, you have been gifted a second life to serve God and humanity. I am coming to America next month, so we will meet soon. Until then, recover and rest as recommended by the doctors.'

A few weeks later, at JFK Airport, we welcomed Swamiji to America. After spotting me from afar, Swamiji rushed towards me. I tried to bow, but he held my arms and embraced me. As he blessed me with his hands, warm tears rolled down my cheeks. Fortunately, I was fit enough to subsequently join Swamiji in his travels around America and the Asia-Pacific. He took every opportunity to express his daily love and care. 'Did you take your medicine?' he would inquire. 'How's the physiotherapy going?' 'Make sure you rest and eat.'

In Sydney, Australia, I observed Swamiji's enthusiasm to interact with youths. Doctors had insisted he not speak due to his heart condition and late age. But Swamiji forgot his health and unreservedly advised the youths for long periods. I recall him speaking in rapid Gujarati for 40 minutes, only pausing for me to translate his insights into English. Throughout the day, he met all the students and encouraged them to excel academically, personally, and spiritually.

In Australia, New Zealand, and Singapore, Swamiji would advise me at night: 'These youths are born and raised abroad. Speak and write to them in English. Encourage them to excel, serve their parents, nurture their values, retain pride in their heritage, and remain connected to God. You must inspire the next generation.'

Today, my guru, Mahant Swami Maharaj continues to be my guiding light. His very presence embodies inspiration, and to earn his blessings is my ultimate goal. He has blessed me dozens of times, placing his hands on my head, back, and throat, imbuing me with noble thoughts, courage, and a voice. Motivated by my guru's dedication, I travel constantly to share his inspiration with the world.

But this book is not about my life; it's about yours. I'm not writing to push my ideas and beliefs or claim I'll transform your life, but to reinforce your conviction that positive change is possible. I firmly believe that when the right wisdom arrives at the right time, it can be truly empowering.

As I travel across the globe, meeting people from diverse backgrounds and hearing their stories, I've come to realize that their most pressing concerns are not the global issues often spotlighted by the media. Instead, it's the everyday struggles that inflict the deepest wounds. It's the battles we face within ourselves, the quest for peace within our own homes, the loss of purpose and identity amidst life's chaos, and the way our priorities and peace are lost in the shuffle of daily challenges. These are the burdens that weigh heavily on our existence.

To improve the world, we must start by shaping our inner worlds. This means not merely seeking peace by closing our eyes, ears, and minds, but by opening ourselves to the dynamic situations around us. We must explore practical ways to embrace daily challenges, rise above them, and find stability within.

This book won't attempt to entice or pull you across each page. Instead, it's intentionally crafted to provide you with the necessary space and freedom to engage with powerful, bite-sized wisdom on a daily basis. We'll explore four areas essential for holistic living: Personal Growth, Family Values, Work Ethics and Human Relations, and Spirituality. You can follow the sequence or dive into the topic most pertinent to you at any given time. I encourage you to read each chapter attentively, absorb its insights, reflect on them, share them, and above all, let those insights become a part of your life.

PERSONAL GROWTH

SECTION 1

PERSONAL
GROWTH

8+8+8

In the relentless marathon of our daily grind, we strive to make progress despite time constraints. Juggling work, family, personal well-being, and long-term aspirations often leads us to wonder: how much can we truly accomplish in 24 hours? We must learn to navigate hurdles skilfully, maintain a steady pace, and ensure that every stride is purposeful. It all starts with a simple formula.

Once in a small county high school, a professor entered the lecture theatre with a sizable glass jar tucked under his arm. As he delicately positioned the empty glass jar on the front table, the students began to whisper amongst themselves in anticipation.

To the students' surprise, the professor pulled out a pile of large stones from under the table, each about the size of a fist. He then carefully placed the stones into the jar one by one until he could fit no more. Turning to the class, he asked, 'Is this jar full?' Students, seeing the jar filled to the top, nodded and replied, 'Of course.'

To everyone's surprise, the professor produced a box of pebbles and began emptying it into the glass jar. Pebbles much smaller than the stones rolled down into the gaps between the stones. Then, again he raised the question, 'Is the jar full now?' Few students hesitated, exchanging glances, while most agreed, 'Yes, now it is full.'

Once again, the professor drew out a bag of sand and poured it into the jar. Tiny grains of sand filled all remaining spaces between the stones and pebbles. And then for the third time, he asked, 'Is the jar full now?' Catching on, all students responded, 'Probably not.'

As a final act, the professor took out a jug of water and poured it into the jar, saturating the sand. 'Now it's truly full,' announced the professor with a chuckle.

Turning to his attentive students, he explained, 'This jar signifies your life. The large stones represent the most important elements. Even if everything else was lost and only they remained, your life would still be full. The pebbles surrounding the stones symbolize the small things that matter. And the sand filling the tiny spaces represents the everyday trivial things that we do in life.'

The professor folded his arms, savouring the silence, until a curious student inquired, 'But Professor, what about the water you poured? Where does that fit in our lives?' To which the professor replied with a twinkle in his eye, 'Ah, yes! The water signifies that no matter how full or busy your life may seem, there is always some room for joy and laughter.' The entire class erupted in laughter at the professor's insight.

In our lives, we often find ourselves juggling between priorities, trying to cram everything into the limited hours of the day. We get so caught up in the hustle and bustle of everyday small tasks that sometimes we forget what truly matters more.

Striking a balance between work and family is a delicate act. Focusing too much on our careers may lead to neglecting family, while simultaneously, the obligation to provide for the family necessitates time and energy. While navigating commitments, prioritizing both personal growth and wellness remains crucial. Yet, caught between home and work responsibilities, we inadvertently neglect ourselves. In this stretched state, it's unsurprising that the pursuit of ultimate goals is inevitably deferred.

The jar of life has limited space, not infinite. In a mere 24-hour day, how much can we truly accomplish? Can we strike a perfect balance and relish the journey to its fullest?

If we wish to be successful in all areas of life, then it starts by creating a basic structure. Let's coin it the 8+8+8 Rule, a distribution of the 24 hours we have in our day.

The first 8 hours of our day are devoted to our professional pursuits. It is imperative to diligently construct our careers, consistently strive for excellence, and above all, maintain a robust work ethic. Incorporating integrity, moral values, self-discipline, a positive attitude, and cultivating meaningful human connections are essential for sustained, long-term success. While accomplishments hold significance, it is how we attain success that truly shapes our character.

The second 8 is dedicated to sufficient rest, as the average time required for a good night's sleep is around eight hours. We must accept that we are not machines but humans, and understand the crucial role sleep plays in our well-being. Quality sleep acts as a rejuvenating force, vital for our mental and physical health. It provides the essential restoration necessary to face the challenges of the upcoming day.

After 16 hours comprising work and rest, we still have 8 hours on our hands. Mastery over this remaining 8-hour period is a game-changer, defining the distinction between ordinary and extraordinary. To remember the priorities within these eight hours, we can use the mnemonic 3F, 3H, and 3S.

3F represents Family, Friends, and Faith.

Our support network, composed of family and friends, flourishes when we invest quality time in fostering trust and open communication. This intentional family time is not only vital for the development and well-being of our children, but also provides meaningful opportunities for expressing affection and appreciation. Moreover, the consistent practice of faith plays a significant role in instilling essential values such as honesty and forgiveness, contributing to the cohesive foundation of our family.

3H represents Health, Hygiene, and Hobbies.

Just as we diligently care for our cars, ensuring the right fuel and regular maintenance for peak performance, it is equally vital to prioritize the well-being of our physical and mental health. These elements play pivotal roles in our overall functionality and performance. Concurrently, the continuous refinement of our character, skills, and intelligence is vital for holistic personal development.

3S represents Service, Smile, and Soul.

As we catapult through life, it's what we give, the way we treat people, and the spiritual pursuit that defines our final trajectory. We must find regular time to align ourselves with our ultimate goals and to pursue a meaningful, purposeful, and fulfilling existence.

As we continue to structure our lives and gain clarity of our priorities, we can begin to build ourselves holistically through practical wisdom.

HEALTHY, WEALTHY, AND WISE

Ever wondered about the secret behind the self-made millionaires, scaling the heights of success, while others settle for mediocrity? What do they possess that others lack? What sets them apart? Surprisingly it starts with a just few simple habits.

In a comprehensive study, Tom Corley, an accountant and financial planner, from March 2004 to March 2007, interviewed 233 millionaires and 128 individuals with lower incomes. Then he spent over 16 months until October 2008 analyzing and summarizing the data.[*]

Among the 233 millionaires surveyed, 177 were self-made millionaires, while 56 had inherited their wealth. Of the self-made millionaires, 105 (59 per cent) had originated

---

[*] Corley, Tom. 2016. *Change Your Habits, Change Your Life*. Hillcrest Publishing Group.

from middle-class households, while 72 (41 per cent) had humble beginnings in poor households.

Corley's research aimed to delve into the lives and backgrounds of these individuals, to study what leads to some people becoming rich while others remain poor. Revealing valuable insights into the paths to wealth and success, his findings reveal the crucial role that habits played in shaping their success stories.

Notably, nearly 50 per cent of millionaires woke up at least three hours before their workday began. This practice underscored the significant role of early mornings in their daily routines. Furthermore, approximately 76 per cent of the surveyed millionaires made daily exercise a top priority, dedicating 30 minutes or more to physical fitness. This commitment to regular exercise highlighted the importance they placed on maintaining a healthy lifestyle.

Additionally, an astonishing 88 per cent of them allocated a minimum of 30 minutes each day to reading, emphasizing the profound impact of continuous self-improvement. An impressive 89 per cent of them ensured they got a good night's rest, with seven to eight hours of sleep each night or more, recognizing the importance of adequate rest for healing and overall well-being.

These findings underscore that it was their daily habits that transformed them into extraordinary individuals, enabling them to achieve remarkable success.

But in an era of instant gratification, it can be challenging to stick to habits and healthy lifestyle choices that may not offer immediate rewards. However, it's worth noting that great legends and individuals who have achieved remarkable success often share a common trait: their dedication to filling their daily routines with constructive habits.

Billionaire Richard Branson, a renowned business magnate and adventurer, reveals his early morning routine as a source of motivation and energy. No matter where he is, he rises early usually around 5 a.m. Branson's mornings are characterized by active pursuits, whether it's playing tennis, going for a walk or run, cycling, or even engaging in the exhilarating sport of kitesurfing if he's near the ocean. For him, the combination of physical activity and the refreshing outdoors sets the tone for a day filled with renewed enthusiasm.

Narendra Modi begins his day well before 5 a.m. Serving as the Prime Minister of India, a nation with a population of 1.4 billion, he is understandably busy. But he daily greets the sunrise with Surya Namaskar, followed by pranayama and yoga to invigorate his body and mind. Thereafter, he immerses himself in meditation. Regardless of his location or the demands of his role, Modi's firm commitment to this daily ritual equips him with the inner strength and clarity needed to confront any challenges that lie ahead.

Well-known tech innovator and founder of Apple Inc., Steve Jobs, was known to practice intermittent fasting and follow a strict diet to improve his mood and overall well-being. His journey towards a healthy diet began when he was a freshman at Reed College, where he discovered a book called 'Diet for a Small Planet' by Frances Moore Lappé.

Inspired by the book, Jobs swore off meat and primarily focused on consuming vegetables and fruits in his diet.

Legendary investor and self-made billionaire Warren Buffett emphasizes that reading has been the most crucial habit he has cultivated. He views reading as a means to continuously update and upgrade himself with new market trends and knowledge, which have played a significant role in his astute decision-making and exceptional financial acumen.

Renowned scientist and physicist Albert Einstein dedicated nine to ten hours to sleep each night. It's postulated that his extraordinary mind required this additional downtime to recharge and maintain its exceptional capacity for creative and analytical thinking.

Whether it's starting the day with early morning vigour, dedicated reading, or even ensuring sufficient rest, these legends recognize the importance of these habits focusing on long-term yield. That is the reason they could carve out time from their busy lifestyles to invest into these healthy habits.

If they can, then what's stopping us? By adopting a similar mindset and commitment, surely we can also pave our way to success and fulfilment.

But where and when do we start?

Let us start small today and build our lives upon the foundation of healthy habits.

1. **Early Rise**: Wake up well before sunrise or rise two to three hours before the workday begins.

2. **Exercise**: Make exercise a priority by dedicating at least 30 minutes a day to moderate or high-intensity workouts.
3. **Diet**: Choose healthy, nutritious, and balanced meal options. Stay hydrated.
4. **Self-Improvement**: Focus on continuous self-growth through constructive habits, like reading useful books, meditation, and self-reflection. Avoid timewasters like aimless scrolling, excessive gaming, or binge-watching.
5. **Sleep**: Maintain a fixed sleep schedule taking adequate rest for seven to eight hours daily.

Undoubtedly, establishing new habits presents a significant challenge. Meeting deadlines, adapting to urgent situations, and managing various responsibilities can disrupt our schedules and undermine the routines crucial for our well-being. However, with dedication, we have the capacity to either resume our habits or adjust effectively to the changes.

I witnessed my guru, Pramukh Swami Maharaj, even at an advanced age, maintain a rigorous schedule, incorporating regular pranayama and meditation. Despite the demands of travelling across multiple villages in a single day, as well as attending numerous assemblies and meetings, he prioritized a daily half-hour walk. When handling a schedule full of travel, Swamiji would stop the car before the destination, and walk the last few kilometres. Such regularity exemplifies the adage, 'Where there is a will, there is a way.'

In his guidance to us, he frequently emphasized, 'To serve others effectively, one must maintain the purity and health of both body and mind.'

Rooted in Indian wisdom is a profound truth that highlights the extraordinary influence of consistency. In the daily rhythm of life, the village women follow a routine of visiting wells every morning to retrieve water. Employing a slender rope, they diligently draw water from the well day after day, gradually leaving lasting marks engraved on the well's stone edge. As time passes, the persistent action of the seemingly gentle rope eventually cuts through the unyielding stone.

So, what prevents us from carving our path to success with firm resolve and an unbroken streak? If we persistently follow this regimen, we are bound to emerge healthier, wealthier, and wiser. Let us take charge of our lives by cultivating these healthy habits and forge a brighter future.

INFINITE SCROLL

Screens and social media have seamlessly woven themselves into our daily routines, providing pathways to connectivity and knowledge through the convenience of pocket-sized devices. However, we cannot deny their addictive allure, the resulting mental fatigue, and the harm to our well-being. Their dual nature, both indispensable and destructive, prompts us to ask: are they a blessing or a curse?

In June 2008, an unassuming Walmart employee named Neil Pasricha embarked on a daily blogging journey, crafting what he aptly named '100 Awesome Things'. In the blogosphere, he was a virtual unknown until post #980, when the readership suddenly surged, and he garnered the attention of major media titans like Wired and CNN. Just a year later, in 2009, Pasricha's blog amassed a staggering 10 million hits, earning him the Webby Award for 'Best Blog'.

But this was only the beginning. Literary agents came knocking on his door, leading him to pen 'The Book of

Awesome', which catapulted him into the ranks of *The New York Times* best-selling authors. This remarkable trajectory underscores the profound influence of social media, where hidden talents can achieve global recognition in a remarkably short time.

Since the advent of social media, our world has undergone an unimaginable transformation. With just a swipe or a voice command, we now have the power to access an abundance of information. We can attend live events taking place anywhere on the planet, establish communities that unite like-minded individuals, harness platforms to promote our ideas, business ventures, and charitable causes, and even pursue education and careers—all from the comfort of our own homes.

Indeed, the advantages of social media are various, but they are not without a flipside. Neil Pasricha, in his book *The Happiness Equation*, openly details the toll of his pursuit of perpetual success. He recalls the grueling three-year grind, his cramped apartment, a sleep-deprived existence, reliance on takeout meals, and the alienation from his friends. His obsession with monitoring his blog's statistics, best-seller rankings, and award nominations left him with a gnawing sense of emptiness. External motivators had taken precedence over his intrinsic goals, eroding his self-confidence. Negative comments, harsh reviews, and the inevitable slip from the best-seller list left him feeling like a failure.

Fortunately, Pasricha eventually recalibrated his priorities, redirecting his focus towards internal goals, while continuing to share his skilled writing and spread positivity to the world. However, many ensnared by the pull of social media are not so fortunate. While countless aspire to achieve online stardom, the harsh reality is that success stories like Pasrischa's are the exception, not the rule.

Furthermore, social media has evolved into an addiction. The same pleasure-inducing chemical reactions in our brains triggered by tasty food are now elicited by our digital interactions. The problem lies in our brain's inability to discern between beneficial habits like exercise and adequate sleep, and harmful habits such as drug addiction or excessive social media use. Consequently, the reinforcement of these chemical responses can lead to addiction.

This outcome is not accidental; social media platforms are meticulously designed to capture our attention and retain it for as long as possible. There is fierce competition among media companies, where your time and data equate to their revenue. One cunning strategy employed by developers is the elimination of stopping cues. These cues function like chapters in a book, signifying a natural stopping point, allowing for a pause or a productive diversion. However, these cues have been eradicated, replaced by never-ending newsfeeds, auto-playing videos, and addictive gaming experiences. While we theoretically retain the ability to cease our engagement, the path of least resistance often leads us to continued consumption.

It is not uncommon to pick up our phones momentarily, only to emerge bewildered and mentally drained, having squandered hours of precious time. For many young individuals, this is not an isolated incident, but rather a daily occurrence, displacing valuable energy that could be spent on education, sleep, and mental well-being. What may seem like fleeting joy is, in reality, a mere form of mental stimulation—screens have stolen our attention, and social media companies have effectively hacked our brains.

The allure of a smartphone has replaced the innocence of traditional toys and the nurturing care of parents. When infants as young as six months old are pacified using screens, we must consider the long-term physical, emotional, and mental repercussions on this generation. What was initially conceived as a valuable tool has now become a dangerous distraction.

Yet, we find ourselves at a crossroads, pondering the ethics of social media. Is it a blessing or is it a curse? In response to such a question, Pramukh Swami Maharaj wisely explained, 'If technology is used with wisdom, then it is a blessing. But without wisdom, it is a curse.'

Much like a knife, smartphones are tools. A sharp knife can be employed to prepare nourishing meals or perform life-saving medical procedures, but in the wrong hands, it can inflict harm, suffering, or even death. We must wield smartphones with caution, entrusting them to individuals who possess wisdom, maturity, and self-control rather than placing them in the hands of children. Much like a knife, smartphones are useful tools, but we must cultivate responsible phone etiquette to regain control.

To this end, we must establish clear boundaries when using our phones by adopting effective habits. Though simple, they can yield substantial benefits to our health and productivity. These habits may include the following:

1. **Designate Tech-Free Zones**: Create specific areas in your home where phone use is not allowed, such as the dining room, bedrooms, or during family meals and activities.
2. **Schedule Screen-Free Breaks**: Incorporate regular screen-free breaks into your day to recharge and connect with the real world.
3. **Set Realistic Limits**: Establish clear boundaries for your phone usage. Define specific times for checking emails, social media, and other digital tasks, and stick to these limits to regain control of your time.
4. **Take Back Control**: Delete unnecessary apps, turn off non-urgent notifications, and make use of your phone's built-in features like 'do not disturb' and digital well-being apps.
5. **Stay Present**: When engaged in conversations, meetings, or studying, give your full attention to the people and tasks at hand. Avoid distractions and multitasking on your phone.
6. **Lead by Example**: Lead by demonstrating healthy phone usage habits and serving as a positive role model for your children. Avoid giving phones to your children.

In 2010, the world witnessed the hype surrounding the launch of the revolutionary iPad. Naturally, journalists clamoured to question the technology visionary and face of Apple, Steve Jobs. When a *New York Times* reporter inquired, 'Your kids must love the iPad, right?' Jobs' response was nothing short of astounding: 'They haven't used it. We limit the amount of technology our children use at home.'

This ironic scenario involves the man behind the trillion-dollar Apple empire, responsible for placing its products in our pockets and homes. Yet, that same man shielded his own children from unnecessary technology usage. This compels us to consider a critical question: What measures will we take to protect both ourselves and future generations?

THE STRESS SOLUTION

In our present-day interactions, while inquiring about someone's well-being—whether it's a stranger, an old friend, a colleague, or a neighbour—a frequent response is: 'life is good', yet accompanied by the admission that it can be quite stressful. It's a shared sentiment that resonates with many. By recognizing stress as a universal aspect of life, we open the door to the opportunity for collective learning and growth, transcending its impact on our lives.

What constitutes the stress that has become so prevalent in our lives?

Stress is commonly characterized as a sensation of fear, tension, depression, emotional strain, or a sense of disappointment emanating from other people, our circumstances, or our thoughts. We grasp the concept of stress not merely from definitions or conversations, but because it's an experience we have all encountered.

In the 21st century, technological advancements have undeniably streamlined our work processes. However, paradoxically, this improvement isn't always reflected in the happiness evident on people's faces. Whether the latest strides in technology have genuinely made the present generation happier than their predecessors is a substantial question, particularly when we find ourselves positioned in a landscape of cut-throat competition and demanding workplaces. Workplace stress permeates our living rooms, kitchens, and bedrooms, while the emotional strains from home infiltrate our offices and meeting rooms.

So, what are the causes of stress?

Several external factors are commonly identified as stressors, such as:

- Physical disability or impairment
- Lack of talent or intelligence, leading to an inferiority complex
- Absence of positivity and inspiration in one's surroundings
- Insufficient support systems, resulting in fear
- Materialistic losses and the inability to make ends meet
- Non-conducive working atmosphere
- Being surrounded by unrelatable people, resulting in loneliness
- Unexpected and unwanted day-to-day occurrences

And the list goes on.

However, upon closer examination of these commonly-cited reasons for stress and a comparison with the lives of certain historic figures—who had every reason to feel stressed but still managed to rise above it—we realize that these external factors alone are not sufficient to define our human experience.

Take the example of Helen Keller. Physically disabled, deaf, and blind, she had every reason to be stressed. Yet, she went on to produce some of the greatest literary works in the world and is known in history for her perseverance against all odds. Consider Nelson Mandela's remarkable journey—he endured 27 years in jail. Despite this, his persistent commitment to equality, coupled with his forgiving nature, left a lasting mark on human rights and served as a global inspiration. And, more recently, look at Pramukh Swami Maharaj, who spent his life enduring daily hardships, regularly travelling to tribal villages in the scorching summer heat to empower the needy. Amid countless unimaginable daily happenings, not once did he appear overwhelmed with stress.

The lives of these remarkable individuals teach us that, despite external circumstances, we too can transcend stress. However, we must first realize that the root of stress fundamentally lies in an unbalanced mind. Inevitably, we find ourselves surrounded by people and circumstances that have the potential to induce stress. However, with mental fortitude, we can navigate and transcend these challenges.

Consider this scenario: You might be seated in a tranquil environment, sipping an aromatic cup of coffee with the comfort of air conditioning. Yet, the enjoyment of reading this book is elusive if your mind is unstable or impatient. Conversely, even in solitude, without food or air conditioning, a stable mind can enhance your overall sense of peace. In essence, the mind stands as the primary source of stress. No external factors—be they people, circumstances, or the atmosphere—can impose stress unless we permit them to do so.

So, how do we cultivate mental strength?

The path to overcoming stress involves developing resilience by adopting positive coping mechanisms and using spiritual wisdom. These skills can be learned and nurtured over time through self-awareness and intentional efforts.

Let's explore this approach in the context of some primary causes of stress:

1. Regrets from past unfortunate events
2. Daily life uncertainties
3. Constant worry about the future

If you find yourself grappling with stress, it's likely connected to one of these factors.

Consider this scenario: Suppose you harbour regrets about not obtaining sufficient education or pursuing a specific qualification. Alternatively, you attribute present fears to a negative incident from your childhood, or you feel ensnared by certain addictions, leading to continual regret. These instances suggest that, subconsciously, you are burdening yourself with your past.

How can you overcome this? The solution lies in not letting the past weigh you down. Learn from it, but resist dwelling on it. Analyze your past, but avoid living in it. This entails the practice of forgiveness towards those who contributed to those negative memories. Failure to forgive and forget only causes harm to yourself. Treat your past with the same pragmatic approach you would adopt for a non-lucrative business opportunity or a minor client—be too occupied with more constructive endeavours to give it undue attention. Just as we behave professionally at work, why not adopt a professional mindset toward your life?

Assuming you've successfully addressed your past, how do you navigate the challenges of the present? Daily life issues can persistently pester you, posing questions about your children, social relationships, or financial concerns.

How can you effectively deal with these challenges? The key is to cultivate a habit of making decisions. You don't need to be a flawless decision-maker, but it's crucial to commit to addressing the problem at hand. Without a concrete decision, the question continues to play in your mind, leading to undue stress. If a specific question cannot be immediately resolved due to unique circumstances or the involvement of multiple people, then give it time. Time often proves to be a robust solution to many problems in life.

In situations where time alone cannot resolve a problem, the next step is acceptance. Embrace an understanding of 'Sankhya Gyan', as explained in the ancient Vedic texts, acknowledging that certain problems in life may never be fully resolved. However, this doesn't mean you allow them to constantly induce stress. By redirecting your attention away from a particular problem, it loses its power to bother you. Similar to how you lock your door to keep thieves out at night, lock your mind to keep those problems out. While both challenges and you coexist in this world, taking control over your focus is the key.

Indian author and journalist, Harkisan Mehta, once explored the relationship between spirituality and stress management in an interview with Pramukh Swami Maharaj.

'You do so much good work for society,' Mehta began. 'Yet when someone criticizes you out of ignorance, misinformation, or jealousy, how does that make you feel?'

Swamiji responded, 'I listen to their criticism and consider: "Are their words true?" If they are true, then I strive to improve.'

'But what if their criticism is wrong?' Mehta asked.

'If their criticism is wrong, then I don't respond or retaliate,' Swamiji replied. 'I pray that Bhagwan (God) blesses them with pure thoughts. Then I forget the person and their words and continue my work.'

Embracing spirituality is fundamental to this process. The ability to transform any situation to your advantage and connect with your inner self emerges when you develop a spiritual inclination in life. Spirituality acts as a shield from the stresses of daily life. As we learn to transcend ego and trust in a higher power, we move one step closer to a stress-free life. Ultimately, at the end of the day, find contentment in your successes, and if something goes wrong, embrace it, learn from it, and let it go. Achieving this equilibrium means that we can remain stable in both the 'good' and the 'bad'.

Even with past and present under control, we may still wrestle with concerns about an uncertain future. Worries about your fate, the well-being of your children, or the potential for untimely family tragedies can be overwhelming. How can you navigate these persistent anxieties? Despite our inclination to believe we wield control over the future, it's imperative to acknowledge that ultimate control lies in God's hands.

Bhagwanji Mandavia, a lead volunteer of BAPS Canada, was diagnosed with leukemia at the young age of 38. While lying in his hospital bed, Mandavia received a letter from a close friend who expressed his sadness upon hearing about the terminal cancer. Though he was too weak to hold a pen, his response came from a place of immense strength and faith. Penning his words, his wife transcribed, 'I accept the doership of God. In my life, I have followed the direction of Pramukh Swami Maharaj, and kept faith in Bhagwan Swaminarayan. I have dutifully cared for my family members, and worked honestly in my professional life. With the grace of my guru, I feel no burden in my heart. I am happy with what God's given me in life. Today, in the last stages of my cancer, I am ready to leave my body to attain my divine destiny in Akshardham. I have no regrets, no worries, no sadness; only joy.'

Ultimately, we must face stress at its three sources—our past, present, and future. Overcoming the past involves forgiveness, learning from experiences, and moving forward. Addressing the present requires developing effective decision-making habits, practicing patience, allowing time to resolve issues, and learning to accept them. Overcoming concerns about the future necessitates maintaining optimism through faith in God. Embracing these techniques in our lives marks the beginning of a journey to transcend stress and cultivate a resilient and peaceful presence.

THE AGE OF DISTRACTION

As we navigate through the second millennium, the challenge to remain focused is met with an evolving range of distractions. Amid the bombardment of notifications and the constant stream of information competing for our attention, there's a growing need to tame the mind.

In 1895, Swami Vivekanand found himself in New York, where he often took evening strolls. One day, during such a walk, his attention was drawn to a group of youths engaged in skeet shooting along the banks of a nearby river. Despite their repeated attempts, the youths consistently failed to hit their targets, prompting a subtle chuckle from Swami.

Upset by Swami's reaction, one of the youths challenged him, asking, 'Have you come to laugh? Marksmanship is no child's play! If you think you're great, let's see you try!'

Taking the firearm in hand, Swami effortlessly and systematically shot down each target, leaving the astonished youths with mouths agape. Intrigued, one youth inquired,

'You seem like an expert marksman. Where did you learn to use a rifle? Who taught you?'

Swami Vivekanand humbly replied, 'My guru, Ramakrishna, taught me that if one learns how to focus, then anything can be achieved.'

Undoubtedly, the ability to remain focused holds boundless potential. Consider the raw power of sunlight; alone, it cannot ignite a piece of cotton. However, when the sunlight is harnessed and intensified through a magnifying glass, directing its focused rays onto a piece of cotton, it quickly ignites. Similarly, as humans, our potential is limitless. However, it's only when we learn to channel our energies through the focused lens of our minds that we achieve magnificent results.

Picture a scenario where we've perfected the skill of maintaining absolute focus on any given task. Tasks that usually take an hour could be completed effortlessly in just ten minutes. Consider attending a lecture once and effortlessly recalling the content during an exam, ten months later. The potential for transformation would be profound.

However, the ability to concentrate is no simple task due to the inherently distractible nature of the mind. Bhagwan Swaminarayan vividly likens the mind to a monkey, persistently distracted and leaping from one random thought to another. Even within the structured environment of a classroom or meeting, our minds tend to detach, meandering wherever their whims may lead, only to return when the session comes to an end.

Staying focused is a challenging skill to acquire. However, it can be cultivated through a disciplined lifestyle and regular practice.

The Mahabharat reveals the extraordinary life of Arjun, who along with his siblings, immersed himself in the teachings of the revered Dronacharya. This master of weaponry and warfare was entrusted with the education of Hastinapur's 105 princes, shaping them into formidable warriors.

In one incident, Dronacharya orchestrated a test to reveal each student's character. A dummy bird perched atop a distant tree served as the target. The conditions were set—release the arrow only upon Dronacharya's command.

After taking a quick look at their postures, Dronacharya waited for some time and then asked the eldest prince, 'Yudhishthir, what do you see?' He replied, 'I see the bird.' Dronacharya continued, 'What else do you see?' He replied, 'Guruji, I see the tree; I see that the branches of the tree are waving in the wind.' Dronacharya was not pleased with his answer, so he moved on to another student. 'Bhim, what do you see?' Bhim replied, 'Guruji, I see so many things. I see the bird; I also see the squirrels playing and running along the trunk up and down. I also see the beehive full of honey.' Displeased, Dronacharya then moved on to another student. 'What do you see, Duryodhan?' He quickly replied, 'I see everything, Guruji. I see the bird; I see the tree; I see the birds flying above the tree; I see you; I see my brothers. I can also see this giant Bhim breathing right next to me.' Dronacharya looked at them and moved ahead in dismay. Some students were quietly murmuring wondering how long Guruji would make them stand in this strenuous posture.

Dronacharya then turned to Arjun. 'Arjun! What do you see?' He replied, 'I see the bird, Guruji.' Dronacharya further inquired, 'Don't you see me, your brothers, or the tree?' He replied, 'No Guruji, I see only the bird.' Dronacharya was delighted to hear this. Dronacharya waited before asking again, 'If you see the bird, then describe it to me. How does it appear?' to which Arjun replied, 'No Guruji, I am only seeing the head of the bird, not its whole body.' On hearing this, Dronacharya was overjoyed and pleased. He promptly commanded Arjun to shoot. Arjun, without any hesitation, released the arrow, piercing the head of the bird.

From a young age, Arjun practiced keen focus with every arrow he released. He made it a habit to rise early in the morning and persistently engaged in archery practice, even during the quiet hours of the night. Steering clear of distractions, he understood their potential to derail him from reaching his desired goal. While his brothers studied under the same tutor, it was Arjun's disciplined lifestyle and nurtured concentration that led him to become the greatest archer.

On 13 May 2006, a young boy approached Pramukh Swami Maharaj in Gondal, a small town in Gujarat. The boy asked, 'How can I concentrate on my studies?'

Swamiji meticulously advised, 'Firstly, don't watch TV. Don't read anything unrelated to your studies. Engage in puja (prayers). Don't waste time wandering or watching unnecessary things. Study hard. Pay attention while reading, keep self-discipline, and control your eating habits. Do not listen to bad things. All these elements will enable you to concentrate.'[*]

Pramukh Swami Maharaj advocated comprehensive child development, endorsing not just academic growth but also physical exercise, social interaction, moral education, and skill development. At the core, he always emphasized the pivotal role of self-discipline and focused effort.

For instance, if one spends half a day binge-watching an online series before commencing work, it's unrealistic to expect those characters and dialogues not to linger in the mind. However, the subtle effects go even deeper—our minds, akin to still waters, mirror everything they absorb, generating ripples of thoughts shaped by everything we see, hear, and consume. While we can't entirely shield ourselves from the world, we possess the power to take realistic steps to minimize negative influences. It's worthwhile to evaluate what our minds consume daily and assess whether it aligns with our long-term goals or desired personal development.

It's also critical to practice concentration in our daily lives. It starts with the small things: giving our full attention during a conversation, silencing phone notifications before picking up a book, or regularly engaging in practices such

---

[*] 'Inspiring Incidents'. *BAPS Swaminayaran Sanstha*, https://tinyurl.com/4nm548vf (accessed 11 November 2024).

as meditation and prayer. By consistently staying focused on each small task throughout the day, and maintaining a disciplined lifestyle, we develop the ability to remain focused during the most significant aspects of our lives.

MASKS WE WEAR

In this age of social media and influencers, people often lead double lives, trapped in the confines of their own fabrication. They craft a public persona, concealing their personal struggles. This stark contrast between their projected image and their inner turmoil serves as a poignant metaphor for the masks they wear. We can learn to shed our masks and become fearless and self-empowered.

Once, a teacher asked his students, 'Whom do you aspire to be like when you grow up?' The students responded with eloquent tributes to celebrities. Their innocent faces glowed as they praised their role models. However, the teacher noticed one student sitting quietly in a corner and asked, 'Henry, who do you want to become when you grow up?' The profound meaning hidden within the young child's reply left the teacher dumbfounded. 'Sir, I want to become myself. I want to become Henry David Thoreau.' That very child grew up to become the renowned writer, poet, thinker, and philosopher we know today as Henry David Thoreau.

By adopting the masks of celebrities, people often lose their own unique identity. I do not deny the importance of drawing inspiration from the lives of great personalities. However, it is crucial not to let their name, fame, or popularity overshadow our own identity. God creates each human being as a distinct individual. In a world with a population exceeding eight billion, no two persons share the same fingerprints, irises, or even the exact pitch and timbre of their voices.

Moreover, nature, temperament, abilities, artistic inclinations, memories, interests, intelligence, and much more—all exhibit diversity and variation. God has bestowed upon everyone a precious gift—their own unique identity. So why should we neglect this great gift and lead a life that emulates another? We should take pride in being our authentic selves.

In 2006, Steve Jobs, the late tech visionary and CEO of Apple, wisely stated, 'Your time is limited, so do not waste it living someone else's life.' Imitating another person breeds hypocrisy, and living a life of hypocrisy fosters speculation.

After the departure of his guru, Yogiji Maharaj, in 1971, Pramukh Swami Maharaj assumed his revered position as the spiritual leader of the organization—a well-known event. Pramukh Swami Maharaj possessed a serious and composed demeanour while Yogiji Maharaj had appeared energetic and cheerful. Referring to that, at one point someone suggested to him, 'Since you have taken the place of Yogiji Maharaj, you should behave like him. You should imitate him.' Pramukh Swami's response should serve as an inspiration to us all. He said, 'That was Yogiji Maharaj's way. If I am not like him, should I simply imitate him? I am who I am, and I do not know how to mimic anyone. I prefer to focus on developing the aspects I lack.'

On 18 September 1998, Ronald Patel, Pulitzer Prize winner and executive editor of the Philadelphia Inquirer, addressed a gathering. He remarked, 'As a journalist, I have posed many challenging questions to Pramukh Swami. Yet, in all his responses, one constant aspect shines through—his purity and sanctity. Regardless of the question posed, the answer is always pure! His words and actions never display a desire for fame. There is no trace of artificiality or hypocrisy. Therefore, the truth of his life has a profound impact on all.'

For the person who does not wear different masks, concerns about personal and public life dissipate. They can lead a life devoid of fear, rising above doubt and suspicion. Indeed, those who feel compelled to wear a mask constantly experience the pressure to uphold their fabricated façade. God has crafted each one of us with unique qualities, and it is only when we embrace our true individuality that we discover how special we truly are.

THE ENDLESS PURSUIT

In our modern society, it is all too easy to get caught up in the pursuit of more. We are bombarded with messages that tell us we need the latest gadgets, the trendiest fashion, and the highest social status to be truly fulfilled. Yet, as we immerse ourselves in this endless chase, we overlook the true essence of a meaningful life.

Imagine yourself at a college reunion, surrounded by your fellow peers reminiscing about the good old days. Suddenly, one of your batchmates arrives in a gleaming new sports car, attracting admiring glances from everyone around. As the engine revs and the car effortlessly zooms by, a blend of awe and envy washes over you. Silently, you find yourself wishing, 'I wish I too had a car like that.'

This longing for more is a universal phenomenon. The bicycle owner longs for an electric scooter, the scooter owner longs for a car, the car owner dreams of owning the latest sports model, and even the wealthy yearn for more power and positions. From aspiring students to business tycoons, all struggle to appreciate and enjoy what they have. Instead, they are constantly consumed by an insatiable desire to have more.

But are we truly free in this pursuit for more? Can we genuinely consider ourselves free while constantly chasing after these desires? Amidst this perpetual cycle of longing, we must pause and ask ourselves a fundamental question: How much do we actually need?

Yogiji Maharaj, the guru of Pramukh Swami Maharaj, explained this through a fable. Once upon a time, in a faraway jungle, a fox woke up to find that the sun had already risen. As he looked at his colossal shadow in front of him, he thought to himself, 'I am so huge, I must eat an elephant to satisfy my enormous appetite.'

Thinking thus, he wandered in the jungle until afternoon. He did try to hunt an elephant but failed miserably. Tired and exhausted, under the flaming hot sun he laid down to rest. As he was resting, he noticed his small shadow and realized, 'Actually, I only need a rabbit but I have uselessly wasted my time and energy chasing an "elephant".'

We too chase inflated desires, and it is because of those that we are stressed as well as saddened. Our desires are like a bottomless well. As we strive to fill it with water, we soon realize that our thirst for more remains unquenched and continues to rise.

William James, one of the most influential philosophers of the Western world, eloquently articulated, 'The art of being wise is the art of knowing what to overlook.'

Throughout history, great personalities have embraced this wisdom. They have found solace and fulfilment by shedding away the unnecessary, realizing that true richness lies in the elegance of a simple life.

Whenever the renowned scientist Albert Einstein was presented with gifts, he would often complain, 'Why are you giving this to me? What kind of chains are you binding me with? I have no need of it and I don't want to be trapped by its lure.' His words echoed his profound understanding that true freedom lies in letting go of unnecessary possessions and avoiding the entanglement they bring.

In 1980, following the groundbreaking success of the SLV-3 (Satellite Launch Vehicle) launch, Dr Abdul Kalam, the visionary aerospace scientist, accompanied Professor Satish Dhawan, the esteemed chairman of ISRO, to meet the Prime Minister of India. What stood out during this significant encounter was Dr Kalam's unassuming attire—simple clothes and a pair of slippers. It was a testament to his remarkable simplicity.

During one of his visits to New York, Pramukh Swami Maharaj required a change to the prescription of his glasses. To address this, a devotee accompanied him to an optician's clinic in Staten Island to get new glasses with the adjusted numbers. The optician suggested placing the new lenses in a new frame. But Pramukh Swami Maharaj replied with a thought-provoking question, 'Do I see from the glasses or from the frame?' Swamiji humbly insisted on keeping his old frame and replace only the lenses.

Swamiji's practical wisdom offers valuable insights into our purchasing habits. The incident prompts us to pause and reflect when we find ourselves enticed by the latest phone model or brand of clothes. Are we buying to address our genuine needs or simply to satisfy our enormous appetite?

In a world that constantly urges us to want more, let us strive to redefine our notions of success and fulfilment. The pursuit of contentment does not lie in an accumulation of possessions, but in embracing a mindset of sufficiency. By cultivating gratitude and recognizing the value of what we already possess, we can free ourselves from the perpetual cycle of longing and bask in the true joy of having enough.

ATTITUDE IS EVERYTHING

In life, setbacks and failures are inevitable shared experiences. While everyone encounters them at some point, the crucial factor lies in how we perceive and respond to these challenges. The way we choose to perceive failures shapes our journey toward success.

In the softly lit living room, Rohit, a student grappling with persistent academic challenges, faced a challenging conversation with his parents following another disappointing exam performance. Rohit's father scowled in frustration. 'Rohit, how did you manage to score so poorly? We've repeatedly stressed the importance of focusing on your studies.'

With a sheepish grin, Rohit began, 'Dad, you won't believe what happened . . . '

His mother, visibly fatigued from countless excuses, interjected, 'Let's hear it, Rohit.'

Rohit continued confidently, 'Well, during the exam, a loud Navratri celebration unfolded in the neighbourhood.

The music and drums were so distracting; I couldn't concentrate.'

His father raised an eyebrow, 'A Navratri celebration, Rohit? That's your excuse?'

Undeterred, Rohit added, 'Yes, Dad, and it gets worse. Our neighbour's house was undergoing renovation, with workers using power tools all day. It was impossible to study in such chaos.'

Rohit's mother shook her head, 'Rohit, this can't continue. You need to take responsibility for your studies.'

Realizing his excuses were falling flat, Rohit tried one more, 'But Mom, you know how noisy it gets in the house with all the chores and commotion during festivals. It's just too hard to focus.'

Much like this anecdote, many of us have likely made excuses at some point in our lives, attempting to mask our shortcomings or failures, perhaps attributing them to external circumstances or other people. Great personalities, however, don't mask failures; they embrace them.

Rahul Dravid, fondly known as 'The Wall' among his followers, stands as one of cricket's greatest batsmen in history. Despite encountering numerous setbacks throughout his career, his exceptional ability to glean valuable lessons from failures paved the way for his eventual success.

Reflecting on his failures, Dravid candidly remarked, 'I am quite qualified to speak on failure, I played internationals 604 times, but I didn't cross 50 on 410 of those occasions. When you fail, you tend to brush a lot of things under the carpet. You try to blame someone, find an excuse. But it's a really good opportunity to learn about yourself.'[*]

In 2007, after a disappointing series against Australia, he faced the setback of being dropped from the one-day international squad. Undeterred, he staged a remarkable comeback in the Ranji Trophy, scoring an impressive 219 runs against Mumbai.

Recalling that challenging phase, Dravid shared, 'We had lost badly in Mumbai and my form wasn't good. I was demoted to No. 6. When I was walking in during the second innings, Steve Waugh said, "Rahul at 6? Next Test at 12?" But I just told myself, "Let me see how many one-balls I can play." It was the simplest thing I could do and it worked.'[†]

Dravid's narrative imparts a valuable lesson on resilience and patient practice in the face of failures. Rather than making excuses, he embraced failures as opportunities for growth, emerging even stronger from each setback.

In life, we often encounter situations that can be perceived in different ways. Some may label them as dreadful, while others find the silver lining even in the most unpleasant of circumstances. Imagine for a moment, a drinking glass with its contents at the halfway mark. Some might sigh and lament, 'It's a shame the glass isn't completely full.' On the contrary, some would gaze upon that very same glass, half-

---

[*] Sudarshan, N. 2017. 'You Need to Learn to Fail Well, Says Rahul Dravid'. *The Hindu*, https://tinyurl.com/2kbwuhm8 (accessed 11 November 2024).
[†] Ibid.

filled, and exclaim, 'Oh, wonderful! I have something to quench my thirst.'

Once, a youth was accompanying Pramukh Swami Maharaj during his spiritual travels in the USA. Upon seeing Swamiji's small accommodation in New York, the youth commented, 'Your room is too cramped, I don't like it.'

Swamiji replied, 'A small room is great. It means we use less power [for lighting or cooling].'

The following week, the same youth commented on Swamiji's spacious accommodation in Toronto, 'Swamiji, your room should always be big, like this.'

Swamiji replied, 'Yes, a big room is great. It means more people can keep me company.'

Now, take a moment to consider: When you face a challenge, what do you see? A glass half full, or half empty? Are we able to remain adaptable and optimistic?

Steve Jobs, the ex-CEO and co-founder of Apple Inc., recounted his remarkable journey in a commencement speech at Stanford University on 12 June 2005. Enduring financial struggles after dropping out of college, he went as far as collecting Coca-Cola bottles for 5 cents each to make ends meet, walking 7 miles every Sunday night for a single decent meal.

At the age of 30, despite holding the CEO position, he faced expulsion from the company he had founded. Reflecting on this pivotal moment, he explained, 'I didn't see it then, but it turned out that getting fired from Apple was the best thing that could have ever happened to me. The heaviness of being successful was replaced by the lightness of being a beginner again, less sure about everything. It freed me to enter one of the most creative periods of my life . . . During the next five years, I started a company named NeXT, another company named Pixar . . . In a remarkable turn of events, Apple bought NeXT, I returned to Apple, and the technology we developed at NeXT is at the heart of Apple's current renaissance . . . Sometimes life hits you in the head with a brick. Don't lose faith.'*

Henry Ford, the founder of Ford Motor Company, aptly encapsulated this sentiment: 'The only real mistake is the one from which we learn nothing. Failure is simply the opportunity to begin again, this time more intelligently.'

On the evening of 10 December 1914, a catastrophic explosion rocked West Orange, New Jersey. The epicentre of this devastating event was the industrial complex of the renowned inventor, Thomas Edison. Ten buildings within his plant, accounting for over half of the site, were consumed by an uncontrollable blaze. Despite the valiant efforts of six to eight fire departments, the inferno, fueled by volatile chemicals, raged on relentlessly, leaving behind a scene of immense destruction and chaos.

Amidst the chaos of that fiery evening, Thomas Edison's response was nothing short of remarkable. As the flames devoured his life's work, he turned to his son, Charles, with an unusual calmness, 'Go get your mother and all her

---

* 2008. 'Steve Jobs' 2005 Stanford Commencement Address (With Intro by President John Hennessy)'. *YouTube*, https://tinyurl.com/2bea2ben (accessed 11 November 2024).

friends. They'll never see a fire like this again.' Charles, understandably concerned, objected, but Edison's wisdom prevailed. He reassured his son, 'It's all right. We've just got rid of a lot of rubbish.'

When journalists converged at the scene, Edison's resolve remained unshaken. He declared to *The New York Times*, 'Although I am over 67 years old, I'll start all over again tomorrow.'[*]

Being true to his word, the very next morning, without laying off a single employee, Edison embarked on the journey of rebuilding.

In 1985, in Ahmedabad, Gujarat, BAPS created a 200-acre township for the grand celebrations of Gunatitanand Swami's Birth Bicentenary. Specifically, the organization enlisted Bengali artisans to craft intricate decorative archways, standing at an impressive 71 feet. These artisans dedicated substantial time, energy, and resources to this monumental project.

However, after just a few days into the festival, disaster struck—a fire engulfed the main grand archway, leaving it half-destroyed. 'How can something that took so long to make, be repaired in just a week? How can it be rebuilt when the artisans have already returned home?' With these questions in mind, leaders and volunteers decided to dismantle the whole archway.

---

[*] 10 December 1914. 'Edison Sees His Vast Plant Burn'. *The New York Times*, https://tinyurl.com/yuz9mt2b (accessed 11 November 2024).

Despite this setback, one individual maintained a positive attitude—Pramukh Swami Maharaj. Where others saw the archway as half destroyed, Swamiji saw a learning opportunity. He gathered the swamis and volunteers, and motivated them to recreate the burnt half of the archway. Despite their inexperience, the volunteers successfully completed the archway in less than a week. From then onwards, now realizing their true potential, archways and other such artistic projects were created in-house by swamis and volunteers.

Whether in the realm of sports, tech, industry, or personal life, these stories demonstrate that in any field, one can encounter setbacks and challenges. What binds these diverse narratives is their shared ability to see the positive side of setbacks and emerge stronger, proving that in the face of challenges, one can truly thrive.

Amidst our adversities, let us not allow excuses to rob us of our future triumphs. Let not failures define us, but let us redefine our notion of success by counting setbacks as the stepping stones towards success.

SEIZE THE DAY

In this fast-paced world, where we are consumed by daily chores, work obligations, and media consumption, where time quickly and quietly slips away, it's not unusual to feel exasperated by the shortness of the day. However, it's not the amount of time that requires our attention, it's how we use it.

Imagine waking up tomorrow to a remarkable gift of $8,640,000 to spend any way you please. You could buy your dream house or the latest sports car. Or you could buy an island or even a private plane. However, there's a catch—any unspent amount will be retracted by the day's end. It's not hard to consider the detailed plans you'd make to utilize this fortune effectively and in its entirety.

In reality, we receive a similar gift each day. God bestows us all with 86,400 seconds, regardless of our circumstances. Nobody gets a little more or a little less. But it's how we value and spend each second that defines our achievements. It's not the quantity of time, but how we use it that truly matters.

Alan Lakein, a renowned American author on time management, famously said, 'Time = life; therefore, waste your time and waste your life, or master your time and master your life.' The way individuals utilize their time truly makes a significant impact on their lives.

History reveals that Mahatma Gandhi devoted his attention to learning the profound teachings of the Shrimad Bhagavad Gita while brushing his teeth. Notably, whenever visitors transitioned during their meetings with Gandhiji, he adeptly organized activities to make the most of those brief intervening periods.

Henry Wadsworth Longfellow, a widely celebrated American poet, creatively utilized his daily ten-minute coffee-making routine to translate half a page of a book. After many years of practicing this habit, he finally gifted the world with the first American translation of the literary masterpiece, 'Inferno'.

On 12 June 1990, Pramukh Swami Maharaj visited Dr Dixit's clinic in Mumbai for a health check-up. While the doctor was preparing the machinery to take Swamiji's X-ray, Swamiji started reading letters from those requesting his guidance. When the time came for the X-ray, he paused his reading; after it was complete, he again went back to the stack of letters to continue reading.

There was a total of five X-rays to be taken. During the one- to two-minute gap between each X-ray, Swamiji returned to reading letters. While the doctor was doing his work, Swamiji was not hesitant to continue his.

Whether in a car, in an assembly, or on a railway platform, whenever he found a moment to spare, Swamiji would read and answer letters. Throughout his lifetime, he read and responded to over 750,000 letters.

In addition to responding to letters, Swamiji's regular day involved meeting scores of visitors, addressing many audiences, visiting at least 20 to 25, and contributing to numerous project meetings. While walking on the treadmill, he would listen to kids' recitations and encourage them. And, while taking lunch, he would listen to the reading of sacred texts.

Despite being busy with multifarious activities, he never complained about lack of time. He consistently found ingenious ways to make optimum use of every second available to fulfil his responsibilities as a spiritual leader, leaving no opportunities untapped in his unwavering commitment to his devotees, all while sparing time to enjoy his favourite activity of offering devotion to God.

The lives of great personalities allow us to reflect upon our own lives. What do we do while we brush our teeth, take our meals, or take daily walks? How do we spend those small moments when waiting to catch a train, or before meeting a friend? How do we spend our time when commuting to our workplace?

Alan Lakein tells us to constantly ask ourselves this question, 'What is the best use of my time right now?'

Remarkably, great individuals never lament the scarcity of time; instead, they strive to utilize it wisely. Let us make little adjustments, form routines, and create a lifestyle where we can make the optimum use of our time, and tap the hidden opportunities that would propel us to become the masters of our lives.

SMOKE AND ASHES

When you consider the biggest threat to humanity, what comes to mind? War? Terrorism? Natural disasters? Global warming? Maybe even artificial intelligence? While these contemporary challenges continue to gain attention, there's a devastating threat we have forgotten about, much closer to home. For too long it's been left unchallenged to freely destroy lives, devour families, and cripple society. It's about time we did something about it.

Substance addiction, including alcoholism, smoking, and drug abuse, stands as a menace to society, yet its immense impact often goes overlooked. According to the World Health Organization, the harmful use of alcohol alone results in the loss of 5.3 per cent of all human lives annually.*

---

* 9 May 2022. 'Alcohol Key Facts'. *World Health Organization*, https://tinyurl.com/djw8mp3d (accessed 11 November 2024).

Moreover, a staggering 237 million males and 46 million females globally grapple with alcohol-use disorders.*

Tobacco, another significant contributor to this crisis, annually claims the lives of over eight million victims. Despite this, 1.3 billion people, constituting 16 per cent of the global population, still continue to use tobacco products.†

Let's put this into perspective. The COVID-19 pandemic shook us profoundly, causing over half a million deaths in India alone.‡ It was a collective trauma that brought nations to their knees. Yet, the harmful impact of tobacco and smoking in India kills more than 1.35 million lives every year—double the toll of the pandemic.§ The irony is stark: while the world rushed to vaccinate against a new enemy, a forgotten one silently claimed double the lives, and continues to do so every year.

Consider terrorism, a word that instills fear and anger. From 1980 to 2023, it claimed 19,866 victims in India.¶ Now, let that sink in. Because every year, smoking kills

---

* 21 September 2018. 'Harmful Use of Alcohol Kills More Than 3 Million People Each Year, Most of Them Men'. *World Health Organization*, https://tinyurl.com/yfr33jbb (accessed 11 November 2024).

† 31 July 2023. 'Tobacco'. *World Health Organization*, https://tinyurl.com/tk5xfd46 (accessed 11 November 2024).

‡ 'WHO COVID-19 Dashboard'. *World Health Organization*, https://tinyurl.com/4b6xx5e8 (accessed 11 November 2024).

§ 30 August 2029. 'Tobacco'. *World Health Organization*, https://tinyurl.com/3m5dwz8z (accessed 11 November 2024).

¶ 5 December 2023. 'List of Terrorist Incidents in India'. *Wikipedia*, https://tinyurl.com/3d49jbek (accessed 11 November 2024).

more than 50 times that amount in India alone.* The comparison is chilling—an enemy we dread versus a habit we have grown complacent about.

So, where's the outcry? Where's the collective rage? Surely the same energy that fueled the fight against COVID-19 and terrorism should be turned towards the battle against addiction. Picture the intensity, the urgency, and the global solidarity we witnessed. Now multiply it by 50, and you'll grasp the scale of the war against addictions.

It's time to let the emotions surge, to feel the weight of those lost lives and shattered families. Substance abuse isn't just a statistic; it's a silent scream that deserves our attention, our anger, and our relentless pursuit of a solution. These numbers represent more than just statistics; each figure corresponds to real people with dreams, loves, and stories that have been cut short.

One such story is of a promising youth from Ahmedabad, Dinesh Patel.† His academic brilliance shone from his early school days. He obtained his bachelor's degree in Electronics Engineering from the L.D. College of Engineering, a prestigious institution in the state, where he consistently earned the title of gold-medallist throughout his years of study. Subsequently, he pursued a master's degree at an esteemed Indian Institute of Technology (IIT), where he

---

* 15 April 2022. 'The Toll of Tobacco in India'. *Campaign for Tobacco-Free Kids*, https://tinyurl.com/4jsnsdt6 (accessed 11 November 2024).
† Name changed to protect identify.

achieved an exceptional academic record, graduating with a remarkable 9.9 out of 10.

His passion for knowledge didn't stop there; he went on to pursue a PhD in Radar Technology. During his research, he developed a radar system capable of detecting a flying object as low as 50 metres above the ground. His work gained recognition when his research synopsis was presented at Harvard University, and NASA extended him a job offer to work in the United States. However, driven by a strong sense of commitment to serve his own country, Dinesh declined the offer and chose to stay in India. The Indian Defence Ministry graciously sponsored his further education.

Given his illustrious academic background, one might expect Dinesh to have joined esteemed organizations such as DRDO (Defense Research and Development Organization), or ISRO (Indian Space Research Organization), or become a defence contractor or consultant to multinational aerospace and defence giants like Boeing or Lockheed.

However, Dinesh's journey took an unexpected turn. He ended up working in a modest fabric processing factory in his hometown, earning a meagre income. How did he transition from a promising student to this unexpected destination? Did we miss out on a critical chapter of his life?

The answer lies in his change of habits. Dinesh's life took an unfortunate turn as he gradually became entangled in the web of alcohol, cigarettes, and drugs. To fuel his costly addictions, he resorted to dipping into his educational funds. His indulgence in drugs and alcohol grew day after day; little did he realize the significant impact his choices would have on his future. In due course, as a review of his underwhelming performance unfolded, the defence ministry conducted an investigation, and he was found in possession of illegal drugs. As a consequence, he was blacklisted, virtually rendering him ineligible for employment.

Dinesh's once-promising journey had taken a sudden and unforeseen turn, unveiling the repercussions of his choices and actions. His story serves as a strong reminder of how many such shining stars are consumed by this unforgiving black hole of addictions.

Realizing the suffering of society, Pramukh Swami Maharaj spent his life passionately campaigning against the use of addictions. He travelled to over 17,000 villages, towns, and cities, counselling addicts and empowering them to reform their lives.

Joseph Muturia, a Kenyan and former member of Parliament, shared his journey of transformation with a crowd of more than a 100,000 people on the grand occasion of the centenary celebration of BAPS in 2007 in Ahmedabad.*

He explained, 'When I came to the 1985 festival [of International Convention for Better Living, Ahmedabad], I brought with me three bottles of Johnnie Walker whisky—one bottle for each day. At the festival, in His Holiness Pramukh Swami's presence, I was to address a meeting. I was drinking, but when I saw Swamiji and the

---

* Swaminarayan Bliss, Swaminarayan Aksharpith, January–February 2008, Vol. 31, no. 1–2, pp. 56.

hundreds of youths renouncing the world to be sadhus, I thought, "If they can give up their whole life, surely I can give up my bad habit."

'So, I promised Swamiji and the entire assembly that I would henceforth stop drinking alcohol. And as I flew off to Kenya, I left my "friend" alcohol forever. Since my vow, 22 years ago, not only have I never taken alcohol, but I have also helped so many people quit smoking and drinking in Kenya.

'On this occasion of Swamiji's 87th birthday, I would like to thank His Holiness Pramukh Swamiji for making my life free of alcohol. But more thankful than me, is my wife. She has sent a letter for me to share with you:

'Dear Pramukh Swami Maharaj, my name is Mrs Jemimah Mogare Muturia. I run a college in Nairobi, and I am doing a PhD in Management. My husband was a drunkard for many years. During the day he worked as an MP and assistant minister, and till late night he used to drink alcohol. Throughout the night I never used to sleep well because I was worried about his welfare. Despite a good government salary, he used to spend so much on alcohol, we didn't have money to buy a house or even pay our children's school fees on time.

'Once, my husband went to India to attend a celebration hosted by you His Holiness Pramukh Swami. He came back full of joy and happiness like he had never been before. I asked him why he was so happy. He said, 'I have left my "friend" alcohol forever.' We rejoiced together and since that time, he has never gone back to drinking. Because of my husband's alcohol-free life, we have been able to afford our own home and further higher education. We have enjoyed a stronger marriage and a more comfortable, healthier, spiritual family life.

'I thank His Holiness Pramukh Swami because through him God transformed my husband's life and my entire family. I also thank His Holiness Pramukh Swami on behalf of many of my husband's colleagues who have quit drinking alcohol because of Swamiji's influence on my husband.'

This is but a single story from the four million lives Pramukh Swami Maharaj transformed. He personally took an interest in individuals from all parts of society, freeing them from a life of addictions and guiding them onto the path of better living.

In 2022, paying tribute to Pramukh Swami Maharaj on his centenary celebrations, BAPS children led a nationwide 15-day de-addiction campaign. After a week's training, 16,000 children from BAPS forums took to the streets, serving approximately four to six hours daily for this cause. Sacrificing their summer vacation, these children personally met over 1.4 million people, of whom over 400,000 pledged to shun their addictions and inspire others to do the same.*

The children also organized exhibitions at various public places spreading awareness amongst society about the dangers of addictions. To conclude their campaign, on World No-Tobacco Day they organized over 100 grand parades with props and floats across different regions

---

* July 2022. Gujarati Bal Prakash by Swaminarayan Aksharpith.

nationally, in which more than 50,000 children participated. Their commendable efforts saved society more than 7.5 billion rupees in direct yearly costs related to substance addictions, and of course, saved hundreds of thousands of families from the clutches of despair.[*]

Furthermore, the campaign also consolidated the children's resolve to never engage in any form of addiction. This is a great example of a generation saved, a generation serving, and a generation empowered.

If millions of people can quit their addictions, then why can't we? If young schoolchildren can walk street-to-street freeing others from their addictions, then why can't we? If we recognize that change is necessary and possible, then we too can shape the world into a more beautiful place.

---

[*] Ibid.

ARCHITECTS OF DESTINY

Gunatitanand Swami Maharaj once said, 'A person is known by the company one keeps.' Truly, our closest connections not only determine who we are, but who we become. From self-made billionaires to world champions and the wise, those at the pinnacle of success have leveraged this truth to draw on the expertise around them and forge their paths. By exploring their stories, we too can elevate ourselves in the presence of greatness.

On 18 December 2022, the collective resolve of 26 footballers took up the ultimate challenge. They patiently proved themselves over time and seized the chance to etch their name in football history as the champions of the 2022 World Cup. But among the elite, one man consistently stood out. At the helm of the Argentinian team was none other than Lionel Messi, commanding presence and admiration alike. Throughout the tournament, Messi not only demonstrated unmatched skill, leading in shots on goal and scoring abundantly, but also emerging as the central figure of his team's strategy. With an innate ability to carve out space, create opportunities, and elegantly orchestrate goal-scoring moves, he truly epitomized what it meant to be a playmaker. As Johan Cruyff, the Dutch football legend, aptly put it, 'Messi is a team player and his individual brilliance is part of something bigger.'[*]

However, Messi's leadership was not just confined to match time. When Argentina suffered an unexpected defeat in their opening game of the World Cup, his fellow players were stunned and in disbelief. As they silently trudged back to the changing rooms amidst the forest of microphones and cameras, Captain Messi stood strong, addressing every question and delivering a resolute message for his country: 'Keep the faith, everyone: we won't let you down.'[†]

As a mentor and friend, Messi earned the trust of his teammates by first trusting in their abilities. When things went wrong, he shouldered the blame, and in success, he shared the credit. Before and after each match, he made a point to appreciate the players, also extending the celebrations to include the coaching staff. Echoing the sentiments of his Argentinian teammates, Cristian Romero fondly recalls the lasting impact of Messi's guidance: 'Anyone who really knows about football knows there is no player like him, but

---

[*] 2015. Cruyff, Johan. 'Lionel Messi More of a Team Player than Cristiano Ronaldo'. *BeIN Sports*, https://tinyurl.com/38xvdxrp (accessed 11 November 2024).

[†] Ibid.

what I will always remember is the kind of person he was with me.'[*]

The significance of positive people cannot be overstated. Friends and mentors arguably hold the greatest sway over our paths. With the right people by our side, we receive invaluable support and constructive feedback essential for propelling us towards success. 'It's important to associate with people that are better than yourself.' Advises Microsoft co-founder Bill Gates, 'Some friends do bring out the best in you and so it's good to invest in those friendships.'[†]

Warren Buffett credits personal success to his friendship with Charlie Munger. Until the age of 35, Munger was practicing law but everything changed upon their first meeting. Buffett reminisces, 'I knew after I met Charlie, after a few minutes in the restaurant . . . that this guy's going to be in my life forever, that we're going to have fun together, make money together, get ideas from each other and we were both going to behave better than if we didn't know each other.'

Munger then left law to pursue investments, and together, they founded the multinational conglomerate Berkshire Hathaway. Their close friendship enabled them to challenge each other's decisions openly. In 1972, Munger imparted a crucial investment lesson, Buffet explains, 'He weaned me away from the idea of buying very so-so companies at very

---

[*] *The Times*, https://tinyurl.com/5d2vytnu (accessed 11 November 2024).

[†] 2017. 'Why Bill Gates and Warren Buffett say your friends are crucial to your career'. *CNBC*, https://tinyurl.com/ean2amaa (accessed 11 November 2024).

cheap prices, knowing that there was some small profit in it, and looking for some really wonderful businesses that we could buy in fair prices.'*

Munger's advice resulted in the $25 million acquisition of See's Candies. Though the candy company had only made profits of about $4 million, under Buffet's leadership, it generated over $2 billion in sales for Berkshire, an enormous return of over 8,000 per cent.[†] Reflecting on their 65-year-long friendship, Buffett explains, 'Charlie has given me the ultimate gift that a person can give to somebody else. He's made me a better person than I would have otherwise been . . . He's given me a lot of good advice over time . . . I've lived a better life because of Charlie.'[‡]

Gunatitanand Swami Maharaj, Bhagwan Swaminarayan's spiritual successor, offers a compelling analogy to illustrate the profound impact of friendship. He likens it to the interaction between wood and stone: if one kilo of wood is bound to ten kilos of stone, the wood is submerged. However, if one kilo of stone is bound to ten kilos of wood, the stone floats. This analogy reflects how the company we keep shapes our progress. Those who encourage us to

* 2023. 'Charlie Munger, investing genius and Warren Buffett's right-hand man, dies at age 99'. *CNBC*, https://tinyurl.com/2vhkbkux (accessed 11 November 2024).

† 2023. Moran, Mark. 'Billionaire Charlie Munger, Warren Buffet's right hand man, dies at 99'. *UPI*, https://tinyurl.com/yzbzr3xr (accessed 11 November 2024).

‡ 2023. 'Charlie Munger, investing genius and Warren Buffett's right-hand man, dies at age 99'. *CNBC*, https://tinyurl.com/2vhkbkux (accessed 11 November 2024).

compromise our values and integrity for short-term gains weigh us down, while the support and guidance of positive role models keep us afloat. It's a matter of sink or swim.

As Buffett wisely remarks, 'Choosing your heroes is very important because you are going to gravitate toward the behaviour of those around you. Associate with people who are better than you are. It will do wonders for you.'[*]

Unfortunately, having a superstar on our team or an investment genius as a business partner is a rarity. However, there may be another avenue. We can find 'heroes' in our parents, family, friends, and teachers. This was the secret behind the success of Dr A.P.J. Abdul Kalam. His journey from poverty to aerospace scientist and then to Indian President was propelled by the lessons absorbed from the people around him.

From his homemaker mother, he learned 'that it does not matter how large or small your sphere of activity is; what counts finally is the commitment that you bring to the job that has ordained to you in this life'.[†] Despite 'many setbacks and defeats', it was the advice of his boatman father that always empowered Kalam 'to look within for strength'.[‡] As a young engineer, Kalam worked with Dr Brahm Prakash who taught him 'how tolerance of others'

---

[*] 2020. Gallo, Carmine. 'Bill Gates: The Most Important Lesson He Learned From 10,649 Days of Warren Buffett's Friendship'. *Forbes*, https://tinyurl.com/5bewst6j (accessed 11 November 2024).

[†] APJ Abdul Kalam. 2024. *The Journey: Transforming Dreams into Action*. Rupa Publications India.

[‡] Ibid.

views and opinions is essential in building teams and accomplishing tasks that are beyond the individuals'.[*] Then as a project director, he credits Prof. Satish Dhawan for showing him 'that a good leader takes responsibility for the failures of his team, but gives the credit to his colleagues'.[†]

From a young age, Dr Kalam actively sought to learn from his surroundings: nature nurtured his scientific curiosity, books connected him to great thinkers, and the people in his life shaped his values. Despite facing a lack of opportunity, Dr Kalam's ability to identify, observe, and imbibe critical life lessons moulded him into the kind, thoughtful, and grounded leader who captured the hearts of a nation. His capacity to connect and learn is perhaps most evident in his relationship with Pramukh Swami Maharaj. Although they met only eight times, Dr Kalam credits Swamiji as his 'ultimate teacher' whose spiritual guidance was transformative. Even at a physical distance, Dr Kalam says he integrated Swamiji's teachings 'of how to love peace, have peace and possess peace'.[‡]

As Gunatitanand Swami Maharaj explains, 'There is a big difference between close association and merely staying together. Fleas reside on a cow's udders yet do not experience the taste of milk. The calf, however, stays at a distance, yet it still gets to taste the milk.' This illustrates that

---

[*] APJ Abdul Kalam. *Transcendence: My Spiritual Experiences with Pramukh Swamiji.* Harper Element, pp. X.

[†] Ibid.

[‡] APJ Abdul Kalam. *Transcendence: My Spiritual Experiences with Pramukh Swamiji.* Harper Element, pp. 17.

it's insufficient to merely be in the presence of good people; we must develop the discernment to identify and appreciate virtues, and then actively apply them to ourselves. To become lifelong learners like Dr Kalam, we must cultivate curiosity, open-mindedness, and dedication. With a growth mindset, we transcend the limitations of time and space.

Pause and deeply consider those who wield influence in your life. Whose advice do you act on? Do their values and teachings shape you into a better person? Have you forged a robust support network? Are you a lifelong learner? And most importantly, whom do you aspire to become? If you wish to harness positivity, ambition, and growth, then remember: mere aspiration won't suffice. You must actively craft the environment around you. Handpick your role models with the utmost care. Once you've found them, cherish them and invest in them, for they are the architects of your destiny.

SECTION 2

FAMILY VALUES

CALM IN THE CHAOS

Geniuses, tycoons, billionaires, and philanthropists are widely celebrated for their success and contributions. However, behind their public facades of jubilant smiles, many are haunted by a dull pain burdening their hearts. Without harmony in the home, even giants crumble inside. Such tragedy compels us to ask: What does it take to transform a house into a home? To find calm amidst chaos? To protect and unite family? Perhaps, the first step begins with oneself.

On a radiant morning, millennia ago, the Kingdom of Ayodhya hummed with activity in anticipation of a grand event. Clouds cut through the towering temples adorned with flags. Colourful ribbons and pennants danced along the streets in the gentle breeze. Chariots and carts raced through royal roads, transporting goods for the festive feast. The city echoed with Vedic hymns and temple bells, and the air grew thick with the aroma of flowers and burning incense sticks.

Citizens eagerly awaited the anointment of the next king, Ramchandraji (also known as Bhagwan Shri Ram).

A short time prior, when King Dasharath saw the reflection of his aged face, he felt the time was right to anoint his eldest son, Ramchandraji, in his place. However, as the designated hour arrived, the king was nowhere to be seen. Despite the ministers' eagerness to commence the ceremony, they remained oblivious to the events that unfolded behind the walls of the grand palace the night before.

Queen Kaikeyi had spent the night imploring the king to designate her own son, Bharat, as the next ruler, bypassing Ramchandraji, the son of another elder queen. Despite the unanimous agreement that Ramchandraji was the rightful and fitting heir to the throne, Kaikeyi, propelled by personal concerns about her social standing, exerted pressure on King Dasharath to fulfil her wishes. With profound dismay, the king felt compelled to bestow his kingdom upon Bharat and reluctantly agreed to banish his eldest son to the jungle for 14 years.

The repercussions of Kaikeyi's actions inflicted such profound pain on the family that it began to engulf them. Dasharath, burdened by grief and guilt, lost the will to live. Ramchandraji's mother, Kaushalya, faced heartbreak and contemplated taking her own life. In response to this distressing situation, Ramchandraji's brother Lakshman declared his determination to reclaim the empire through force. Lakshman's twin, Shatrughna, in search of someone to blame, sought retribution. Even Bharat contemplated disowning his mother, Kaikeyi. The dire situation seemed to be spiraling toward revenge, violence, and chaos. Tragically, one person's selfish desire was poised to destroy the entire family.

However, amidst the turmoil, there was one person who remained stable: Ramchandraji. While his family members attempted to navigate the painful situation through escapism, force, or blame, Ramchandraji adopted the path of patience, tolerance, and forgiveness. Embracing the challenging circumstances with humility, he provided support and guidance to his distressed family. Through a foundation of love, trust, and mutual respect, they were able to set aside their grievances and navigate the difficulties together. Despite a further 14 years of trials and tests, they all found strength and hope in Ramchandraji as a central figure until the joyous moment when they could finally reunite in Ayodhya once again.

Spanning across millennia, the Ramayan, depicting the life of Bhagwan Shri Ram, continues to resonate with the masses as it imparts universal lessons relevant to our contemporary lives. Despite the immense wealth, prestige, talent, intelligence, and nobility within the royal household, they were, at their core, still a family. Similar to all of us, when our families experience conflict, our well-being is affected, irrespective of personal and professional success. Our personal peace is intricately connected to that of our families. Therefore, fostering the well-being, progress, and harmony of our families is as crucial as other priorities in our lives.

Fascinatingly, the Ramayan delves into a profound inquiry: what should be our course of action when everything goes wrong? At times, despite our sincere attempts to protect our families, unforeseen challenges—whether it be a financial crisis, conflict, or, as seen in Ayodhya, a relative's grievous mistake—can afflict those we hold most dear. What steps should we take then? In the Ramayan, despite the relentless attempts of relatives to persuade Kaikeyi, their efforts fell on deaf ears. She remained stubborn, even when it posed a risk to the well-being of her family and, by extension, herself. While engaging in damage control and conducting constructive dialogue are crucial, what do we do when the solution proves elusive?

Mahant Swami Maharaj frequently imparts his blessings to newly-wed couples, emphasizing, 'One should always consider, how can I be the perfect husband? Or how can I be the perfect wife?' Swamiji encourages individuals to refrain from placing heavy expectations on their partners and, instead, to focus on excelling in their own unique roles. Both spouses mustn't anticipate having flawless partners. Rather, dedicating themselves to becoming the best version individually can lead to heightened happiness collectively within their family.

Bhagwan Shri Ram stands as an exemplary figure, cultivating remarkable patience as he excelled in his roles as a son, husband, and brother, even in the face of Kaikeyi's challenging behaviour. Furthermore, his stability, support, and guidance empowered other family members to become the best version of themselves. By becoming the unifying force in our families and offering steadfast support, we can guide our families toward peace even in the most challenging of times.

But how can this be achieved? On 28 June 2007, Daniel Cook, an industrialist from Utah, sought blessings from Pramukh Swami Maharaj and posed a question. 'How can I become an ideal father and husband?' Swamiji responded, 'To achieve this, you must observe morality and maintain harmony within your family. Foster love between you and your wife by learning to compromise. Spend quality time with your children and wife. Make it a daily practice to sit together with them and engage in family discourse. Cut down on TV time; instead, sit with your family and read good books.'

Even as a detached swami, Pramukh Swami Maharaj lived within society, extending guidance to innumerable families. During his lifetime, he read and responded to 750,000 letters, and visited 250,000 homes. He attentively engaged with long stretches of people each day, guiding diverse family, work, and life-related matters.

Revealing the essence of happy family life, he emphasized key points for family harmony:

1. Follow a value-based life, incorporating principles such as integrity, faith, and forgiveness.
2. Cultivate constructive habits.
3. Allocate quality and regular time for your family.
4. Foster effective communication, compromise, and support.
5. Teach these lessons to your children.

Certainly, achieving these goals requires dedicated time and effort. It requires making family life a top priority and a strong commitment to the regular study and practice of these lessons. But quite simply, we start this profound journey with one daily thought: 'Let me become the best I can be.'

'WHY SHOULD I?'

'**P**ersonal progress is shaped by how we perceive and understand others.' This wisdom, shared by Mahant Swami Maharaj, encapsulates a fundamental truth about the human experience. Amid the sanctity of homes, strain, blame, and conflict often emerge, stemming from misunderstanding. Such turmoil can exist even between siblings, like twin brothers, Sagar and Aakash.

They were at it once again! Sagar and Aakash were engaged in a relentless exchange for the past thirty minutes. It was a bizarre sight, a face-off between two identical twins. Not only because they were mirror images of each other, but because their connection extended beyond mere physical resemblance. They shared a profound bond and often found themselves in sync: thinking, acting, and speaking in unison. Yet, amid this harmony, the refrain of 'Why should I? Why can't he?' resounded loudest. These questions, typically sparked by their parents' pleas for one of their children to complete a chore, often ignited arguments so long that it obscured the initial cause of contention. Despite the twins' deep bond, their disagreements puzzled their parents. They wondered why such strife arose between two individuals so alike in many respects. Slowly it became apparent that beneath the brothers' similarities lay individual perspectives as distinct as their fingerprints. The twins both felt the sting of perceived discrimination when tasked with responsibilities. In this fogged mindset where rationality gives way to discord, each was convinced of their own righteousness and the other's lack of understanding.

Their debates mirror the age-old problem of whether the figure before them is a six or a nine. Viewing from one side, Aakash insists it's a six, while opposite, Sagar argues it's undoubtedly a nine from his. Both are correct, yet their unwillingness to concede ground keeps them locked in ongoing disagreement. The core issue lies not in their differing perspectives, but in their reluctance to step into each other's shoes. This inflexibility, if persistent, ensures they remain poles apart despite their inherent similarities. If such division disturbs twins, then what of the broader world with its diverse individuals, each shaped by unique circumstances and experiences?

With a staggering eight billion humans inhabiting the planet, the diversity of perspectives is phenomenal. From birth, we are thrust into a kaleidoscope of backgrounds, beliefs, and ideologies. Yet, amidst this variety, a common thread binds us: the need for communication and understanding. Interaction is fraught with complexities akin to deciphering a never-ending string of sixes and nines. The human mind, a tangled maze of thoughts and emotions, craves connection and meaning. To achieve this, cooperation is paramount, and conflict resolution is an essential skill.

Accepting differing viewpoints does not necessitate forsaking one's own beliefs; rather, it recognizes the depth and diversity inherent in human thought. It is perfectly natural for Aakash and Sagar to hold different perspectives, given their unique identities as individuals. However, if they aspire to learn the complexities of life, they must cultivate an understanding and appreciation for each other's viewpoints.

The objective is not to impose one's perspective onto another, but to genuinely learn and respect the stance of others. This requires a shift away from efforts to change someone else's viewpoint unnecessarily. Instead, the focus should be on fostering mutual understanding and respect. Progress is made when individuals extend a hand towards one another, embracing different perspectives. Curiosity and openness can build bridges of understanding that transcend cultural, ideological, and interpersonal differences. Through this celebration of diversity, deeper connections are forged.

What our homes truly need is empathy. This goes beyond mere recognition of another person's emotions; it entails stepping into their shoes and seeing the world through their eyes. Aakash and Sagar, despite their shared experiences, possess distinct viewpoints shaped by their different life journeys. Through the practice of empathy, they can begin to understand and respect each other's perspectives. This demands an openness to listening without bias and a willingness to validate each other's emotions. When Aakash empathizes with Sagar's frustrations and concerns, and vice versa, they create an environment conducive to genuine dialogue and reconciliation. This forms the bedrock upon which their relationship can flourish despite their inherent differences.

Furthermore, effective communication plays a crucial role in bridging the gap between conflicting perspectives. It encompasses articulating one's thoughts clearly and attentively listening to others with an open mind. Aakash and Sagar must cultivate the ability to express themselves openly while also refraining from defensive or hostile reactions. By engaging in constructive dialogue, they can delve into the root causes of their disagreements and strive to discover common ground. This necessitates a readiness to compromise and a dedication to comprehending each other's underlying motivations. Through patient and respectful communication, they can gradually dismantle the barriers that divide them.

Moreover, embracing diverse perspectives demands a readiness to confront our own biases and prejudices. This entails critically examining our beliefs and assumptions, and being willing to challenge them when necessary. Aakash and Sagar need to acknowledge that their differences are not inherently divisive, but rather opportunities for personal growth and collective understanding. They should ask themselves: 'Am I misreading his intentions?' 'Am I expressing myself properly?' 'How do I avoid conflict?' 'What can I do to help the situation?'

Embracing diverse perspectives presents formidable challenges. Biases, cultural disparities, and power dynamics often obscure the path to genuine understanding. Nevertheless, meeting these obstacles with humility and resilience can lead to profound growth and reconciliation. As the Swiss psychiatrist, C.G. Jung, insightfully observed, 'Everything that irritates us about others can lead us to an understanding of ourselves,'* implying that our interactions with others serve as mirrors for self-improvement.

Mahant Swami Maharaj illustrates this concept with the analogy of a person with a smudge of dirt on their face. When they see their reflection in the mirror, they mistakenly attempt to clean the mirror instead of their own face. Similarly, we often project our flaws onto others and critique them instead of striving to improve ourselves. While there are times when our role as parents or mentors requires us to teach others, our primary focus should always be on self-improvement. Instead of imposing our opinions, why not seek to understand first? Instead of disciplining others, why don't we prioritize controlling our own anger first? If we aim to help others, we must first learn to help ourselves.

Mahant Swami Maharaj often emphasizes, 'It's not about "who is right", but "what is right" that matters most.' This suggests that even if you believe the other person is wrong, it is not worth jeopardizing your relationship over

---

* C.G. Jung. 1961. *Memories, Dreams, Reflections*. pp. 246.

a trivial matter. We should prioritize unity and peace over our need to 'be right' or protect our ego. Wouldn't it be more beneficial for Aakash or Sagar to perform an extra chore instead of engaging in conflict? While the responsibility may not be evenly shared, isn't their brotherly bond more valuable than mere fairness? Surely, patience, empathy, humility, and effective communication are more constructive ways to facilitate learning than engaging in arguments.

Mahant Swami Maharaj eloquently states, 'Unity is God's power,' signifying its essence not only as a spiritual practice but as the ultimate catalyst for a harmonious world. As Aakash and Sagar journey towards reconciliation, they epitomize this timeless value. Their readiness to embrace diversity and cultivate connections lays the groundwork for a more compassionate and equitable society. Ultimately, the question transforms from 'Why should I?' to 'Why shouldn't I?' or even 'How could I not?' By embracing empathy, communication, and self-awareness, we open the door to a world where differences are celebrated, and unity prevails.

THE SMOULDERING LOG

In the media, in our professional lives, and particularly within our homes, negativity seems to suffocate us at every turn. We tend to gravitate toward the trials, tribulations, and grievances of everyday existence. This toxic behaviour drains our spirits and clouds our outlook on life. It's time to flip the switch and become the beacons of positivity we were destined to be.

It begins at home. Small things start to irritate us. Perhaps it's a spouse leaving dishes unwashed, a son running late for school, or a daughter making unreasonable demands. They say familiarity breeds contempt. Have you ever noticed how if you have food stuck between your teeth, your tongue naturally gravitates towards that spot? The other thirty-one teeth are fine; in fact, all thirty-two have been serving you well until now. But today, that one spot is getting on your nerves. Similarly, within our own homes, our loved ones possess many positive qualities. Yet, when they act contrary to our expectations, it can disturb us greatly. Suddenly, it's easier to focus on that one flaw, even amidst dozens of good qualities.

And what follows? As our focus intensifies, we unwittingly immerse ourselves in a state of suffering, burdened by the weight of negativity. Ultimately, we're left drained, fatigued, and disheartened. Bhagwan Swaminarayan offers a poignant metaphor, likening a negative mindset to a half-burnt log, constantly smoldering.* Though the flames may not be visible to the eye, the lingering smoke of discontent remains. Have you ever caught yourself grumbling about perceived grievances during your commute? Or spent sleepless nights mulling over perceived mistreatment at home? The half-burnt log persists in its smoldering, consuming us from within.

This type of negative thinking not only damages your well-being and behaviour but also shapes your interactions with others. Chronic, long-term stress, like that stemming from constant complaining, has been shown to have detrimental effects on the brain, particularly on regions associated with memory and reasoning. Simply put, maintaining a positive outlook and surrounding ourselves with positivity can bolster our ability to ward off diseases.†

---

* Sahajananda, Swami. 2014. *The Vachanamrut: Spiritual Discourses of Bhagwan Swaminarayan*. Section Gadhada I 28, Contributors: Bochasanvasi Shri Aksharpurushottama Sanstha, Swaminarayan Aksharpith (2nd ed.). Ahmedabad.

† Parton, S. *The Science of Happiness: Why complaining is literally killing you*, https://tinyurl.com/bdcb8d3t (accessed 11 November 2024).

Stanford psychologists carried out an experiment where they took 104 individuals and split them into two groups.[*] One group was tasked with writing about a time when they felt bored, while the other group was instructed to reflect on instances where they perceived life as unfair or when they felt wronged by someone. Afterward, participants were approached to assist researchers with a simple task. Surprisingly, those who had written about negative experiences were less inclined to offer help.

In a similar study, participants who adopted a victim mindset—feeling wronged by others—displayed tendencies toward selfish behaviour. They were more likely to leave behind litter or steal pens belonging to the researchers. Simply dwelling on negative incidents, whether directed inwardly or toward others, influences our behaviour in daily interactions. Some studies even suggest that negativity heightens aggression toward individuals who may not have even been involved in the original situation.[†]

It all boils down to our personal attitude. The more negative our mindset now, the more likely we are to perpetuate negativity in the future. As Nishkulanand Swami, a celebrated poet and prominent disciple of Bhagwan Swaminarayan, aptly wrote, 'It is not your responsibility to correct others; just improve yourself.' This insight is crucial

---

[*] Zitek, E. M., Jordan, A. H., Monin, B., and Leach, F. R. 2010. 'Victim entitlement to behave selfishly'. *Journal of Personality and Social Psychology*, pp. 98(2), 245.

[†] Din, N.S.B.M., and Ahmad, M. 2021. 'Emotional Regulation on Negative Affect and Aggression: A Review'. *Asian People Journal (APJ)*, pp. 4(2), 29-44.

because it underscores the importance of prioritizing self-improvement rather than attempting to first change those around us. Our perception of the world is a reflection of our internal state, and positivity is an internal trait that can be nurtured. The process begins by actively seeking and acknowledging positive qualities in others.

Simply find that one virtue. Remember it, appreciate it, cherish it, and share those moments. When people make mistakes, remind yourself of the times those individuals brought joy or assistance into your life. By believing in the goodness of others and treating them positively, we can expand that circle of positivity into the environment around us. Each of us holds the responsibility to cultivate a positive environment in our homes. To do this, we must first nurture a positive environment within our own minds.

Within the Babemba tribe of South Africa, when someone behaves irresponsibly or unjustly, the community responds in a remarkable way. The accused individual is placed at the centre of the village, bringing all work to a halt, while every member of the community—men, women, and children—gathers in a large circle around them. What do they do? Do they shout, scold, or punish?

No. Each person in the tribe takes turns speaking to the accused, recalling the positive aspects of their life. Every act of kindness, strength, and generosity is recounted in detail. They remind the individual of their inherent goodness and love. Surprisingly, this tribal ceremony doesn't conclude after just one evening; it often extends for several days. Finally, the tribal circle is broken, and a joyous celebration ensues as the accused is warmly welcomed back into the tribe.[*]

The Babemba tribe holds a profound belief in the inherent goodness of people, understanding that negative action may simply be a cry for help. They advocate that the most effective defence against perceived negativity is positivity. Punishment and retaliation, they assert, only serve to bury the inherent goodness within individuals, sometimes forever. They recognize that those who commit harmful acts are not inherently bad people; rather, they may have lost sight of their true nature. Choosing compassion, the tribe strives to remind family of their inherent goodness.

In our modern, fast-paced society, forgiveness often eludes us. Yet without it, genuine peace of mind remains elusive. By fixating on a single misdeed, we reduce an individual's identity to their mistakes, rather than acknowledging the wealth of positivity that defines them. Embracing this perspective not only brings personal peace, but also spreads positivity to the environment around us.

Mahant Swami Maharaj is a shining example of the power of positivity. He actively encourages those around him to focus on the good. Wherever he travels, he initiates regular sessions during his mealtimes where local congregations gather and collectively present and appreciate one another. During these moments, Mahant Swami Maharaj attentively listens to every virtue, savouring each word with each bite, often becoming so engrossed that at times he even forgets

---

[*] Kornfield, J. 2008. *The Art of Forgiveness, Lovingkindness, and Peace*. Bantam.

to eat. As he hears about the positive qualities of individuals, his eyes sparkle, a broad smile beams across his face, and he reverently acknowledges the divinity within them with folded hands and a bow of respect. In the days that follow, he continues to reflect on these positive qualities during his daily routine.

Remarkably, even decades later, I have witnessed him recall these virtues upon encountering the individuals once again. This practice of affirmation cultivates a culture of mutual respect, support, and appreciation, leaving a lasting impression on all those present. Those who have experienced these divine moments cherish them for a lifetime. Mahant Swami Maharaj's positivity is a source of enduring peace and inspiration—an inherent state that profoundly influences the world around him.

We, too, can adopt such a practice, starting within our own homes. Gathering as a family a few times a week, we can actively express appreciation for one another and acknowledge each person's contributions. Another delightful approach is to write thank you notes to our loved ones and discreetly hide them in unexpected places, like little treasures waiting to be discovered. These thoughtful gestures of appreciation have the power to brighten their day and uplift their spirits in unexpected ways.

Research suggests numerous benefits from such exercises, especially for young minds. They promote a positive perspective on life, instil self-confidence, and empower people to confront challenges. Moreover, those surrounded by positive narratives tend to experience fewer irrational negative thoughts and exhibit fewer symptoms of depression.* So, let's embrace these benefits by spreading positivity to the world around us. Remember, it all begins at home.

---

* Burnett, P.C. 'Self-talk in upper elementary school children: Its relationship with irrational beliefs, self-esteem, and depression'. *J Rational-Emot Cognitive-Behav Ther.* pp. 181–188.

WAR OF WORDS

In a world that celebrates freedom of speech and expression, where even the quietest voices from the most remote corners are amplified across the globe, and where online communities ignite movements and challenge governments, we seem to have overlooked a fundamental human value: with freedom comes responsibility. Our words can heal or harm, unite or divide. Often, the distinction hinges on a single pause—a brief moment of reflection—before we speak.

'Oh, welcome, Your Royal Highness!' Grandad mocked with a sarcastic bow. 'King Neil, please, grace us with your presence. Should I roll out the red carpet?' Grandad had a habit of venting his frustrations on his family through a stream of insults, and today it was Neil's turn, all because he was late. Familiar with Grandad's unpleasant attitude, Neil quietly headed to the kitchen, where his mother, Megha, was waiting to comfort him and help defuse the tension.

However, this only served to fuel Grandad's anger. 'Stop coddling him, woman! Grow a backbone!' he snapped, redirecting his harsh words at Megha. 'Teach him some manners for once, or he'll end up like his good-for-nothing father!'

Seven-year-old Priya watched the scene unfold with curiosity before retreating to her bedroom. Once there, she lined up her dolls and started venting her frustrations at them, mimicking Grandad's harsh tone. Although she didn't fully understand the meaning of the words, she quickly picked up the angry mannerisms and repeated them.

Priya's high-pitched voice reached Megha in the kitchen. When she looked into her daughter's bedroom, she was taken aback to see Priya mimicking Grandad's angry tone. Disturbed by what she saw, Megha quietly took Grandad by the hand and led him to Priya's room. There, he saw Priya pointing and shouting at her dolls with the same harshness he had used. Grandad's jaw dropped as he recognized his own words coming from his granddaughter.

He left the room, feeling a wave of regret wash over him, and slowly walked to the kitchen, where he dropped into a chair, the burden of guilt pressing down on him. As Grandad held his face in his hands, he began to reconsider his behaviour. His sharp words weren't just hurting the people he loved—he was unwittingly teaching them to do the same.

The word 'vaani' comes from Sanskrit and refers to the human capacity to communicate thoughts, ideas, and emotions through speech. Speech is one of the defining traits of humanity; no other species on Earth communicates quite like we do, making it a crucial component in the advancement of civilization. However, as with any tool, its impact depends on how it is used. A knife, when used properly, is a valuable kitchen tool for cutting fruits and vegetables or a surgical instrument for doctors performing operations. Yet the same knife, used improperly, can cause significant harm.

Similarly, 'vaani'—speech—can be a force for healing or harm, for unity or division, for empowerment or oppression. The way we choose to wield our words can build bridges or burn them, uplift others or break them.

Until he saw Priya repeating his words, Grandad had never truly grasped the impact of his speech. He knew his words could be hurtful, but he didn't realize just how deeply they could affect those around him. It was only after witnessing his granddaughter mimicking his harsh tone that he began to understand the far-reaching consequences of his behaviour.

This is why 'vaani' is incomplete without 'vivek.' Vivek—derived from Sanskrit—refers to the ability to discern right from wrong. Just as a skilled surgeon uses a knife to heal rather than harm, 'vivek' guides us to use our words for positive, constructive purposes rather than causing pain or damage. Without vivek, even the most eloquent speech can become destructive. It is the balance between these two—thoughtful discernment and the power of speech—that allows us to communicate effectively while minimizing harm.

In the vast expanse of our minds, thoughts come and go like waves in the ocean—some crashing onto the shore, others receding into the depths. This natural filtering system, though often taken for granted, is crucial for maintaining harmony in our world. Imagine a reality where everyone voiced every single thought without restraint, hurling insults without cause and spewing every superficial idea that crossed their minds. Relationships would shatter, workplaces would collapse, and social cohesion would crumble under the burden of unfiltered expression.

A discerning mind guided by 'vaani vivek' serves as a compass for navigating moral complexities, allowing individuals to make informed choices. This principle filters words before they're spoken, considering context, timing, audience, and potential impact. When these filters fail, words can become dangerously powerful, often causing harm and destruction. History is filled with examples of the catastrophic results of careless speech.

While some people naturally possess this virtue, others need to develop it through practice and conscious effort. By increasing self-awareness and observing individuals who exemplify 'vaani vivek,' anyone can internalize these values and improve their communication skills.

Grandad could have paused to consider the impact of his words before launching into a tirade. He could have noticed that there was a young girl in the room and realized that his harsh words would cause his family pain without providing any real solution. When we let emotions drive our reactions, we often lose the opportunity to find constructive outcomes. Grandad's goal was for his grandson Neil to come home on time. If he had approached the situation calmly, he could have discussed the reasons for Neil's lateness and worked together on a solution. Instead, by giving in to his anger, he ended up creating tension and reducing the chance of resolving the issue positively.

The quality of communication, not the quantity, is paramount in fostering meaningful connections. Within the Swaminarayan Faith, analogies such as using speech like milk or ghee instead of water are used to emphasize that one's words should be carefully chosen and used only when appropriate, rather than being utilized indiscriminately. Mahant Swami Maharaj outlines four simple steps to cultivate positive communication.

Firstly, at the core of every conversation is a simple yet profound concept: 'wish for their best'. This means approaching every interaction with genuine warmth and pure intentions, by mentally wishing the best for the person you're speaking with. It's like offering a friendly handshake or a warm hug before diving into the actual conversation. By setting this positive tone, you create an environment where trust can grow, and where people feel valued and respected from the outset. This approach doesn't rule out serious discussions, but it emphasizes that the goal of the conversation is to benefit the other person rather than to bring them down.

Next comes 'humility'. This is a gentle reminder to set aside our ego when we speak. Regardless of our age, position, or intellectual superiority, we should always maintain respect—not merely as a social courtesy, but because everyone has something valuable to offer. When we approach conversations with humility, we no longer see ourselves as above others. As a result, differences start to fade, and we open our hearts and minds, leading to richer conversations and new learning opportunities.

'With discretion' teaches us to consider the ripple effect of our speech. Every word we utter has the potential to shape someone's day, influence their decisions, or even impact their overall perspective on life. Whether we're offering praise or delivering criticism, it's crucial to choose our words carefully as well as consider the right timing and tone. It's also important to look at the broader context and evaluate the long-term impact beyond the immediate situation. The same message, depending on how it's worded—with or without discretion—can have vastly different outcomes, ranging from harmonious to polarizing. This step would have been particularly valuable for Priya's grandfather, who could have avoided creating tension with more careful speech.

Finally, there's 'without negatively impacting their life'. Some situations require firm words, but even when addressing a problem, we can do so in a way that lifts people rather than tears them down. Before engaging in difficult conversations, take a moment to ensure your intentions are focused on helping, and consider asking for guidance so that your words are received without causing harm. Approach these talks with support, encouragement, and a touch of kindness. By speaking with empathy and understanding, we create a world where everyone feels valued and supported.

Once, Indian author and journalist, Harkisan Mehta, inquired about the practical application of 'vaani vivek' in managing difficult situations. During an interview with Pramukh Swami Maharaj, he asked, 'You lead a global organization with numerous charitable and spiritual activities, while managing hundreds of swamis and thousands of volunteers. When the people you manage make a mistake, do you reprimand them?'

'Yes, sometimes I must address their mistakes,' Swamiji calmly replied, 'However, when I do, I ensure it is in a manner that uplifts them rather than discourages them. My approach is to use words, tone, and care so they understand their errors without feeling hurt, depressed, or guilty. I nurture their enthusiasm, encouraging them to improve personally and spiritually, in addition to continuing their service.'

Practicing these ideas with self-awareness can transform them from passive thoughts into active habits. Whether it's a conversation with a neighbour, negotiations with a business partner, or a disagreement with family, these principles foster effective communication. This approach leads to interactions grounded not just in short-term emotions or reactions, but in long-term benefits and positive outcomes.

Ultimately, 'vaani vivek' holds the key to creating a world of harmony, where mindful communication fosters understanding, compassion, and unity. This practice encourages us to pause before speaking. In that brief moment, there's an opportunity to reflect on the value of the words yet to be spoken: 'Is it necessary to say what I am about to say?', 'Is this the appropriate time and place?', 'Is this the right audience?', 'Will my words hurt or benefit others?', 'Will I later regret saying this?' By contemplating these questions, we can ensure that our communication heals rather than hurts. As Priya navigates her formative years, there's hope that Grandad, too, can embrace this approach, positively shaping Priya's future through his words and actions.

QUALITY FAMILY TIME

In the hustle and bustle of our modern-day lives, the concept of family often takes a backseat to the demands of work, school, and various other responsibilities. Nevertheless, the value of familial bonds cannot be overstated. Despite the scarcity of time, it is crucial to diligently seek and wisely utilize it. After all, timeless moments are not simply gifted; they are consciously created. Family transcends mere blood ties; it is defined by the connections that resonate within our hearts and are reinforced through shared routines and experiences.

The doorbell rang with a soft chime, and the front door swung open. A man trudged in, his shoulders sagging with the weight of a long day at work. He collapsed onto the sofa with a sigh, letting the cushions swallow him whole. 'Dad's home!' A little boy burst into the living room, bouncing excitedly, and then settled into his father's lap. 'Dad, why did you come home so late today? I've been waiting for you all day! Can we go to the carnival tonight? There's a parade and everything!'

His father smiled, though it didn't reach his tired eyes. 'Not tonight, buddy. I'm really exhausted.'

'But you promised!' The boy's voice grew loud with frustration. 'You always say you're tired!'

From the kitchen, his mother called out, 'Give him a break, sweetie. He's had a long day. Why don't you get him tea first?'

'Okay,' the boy mumbled, reluctantly sliding off his father's lap. He fetched a cup of tea and handed it to his father, who took a grateful sip.

Grandpa, sitting in his usual spot by the window, suggested, 'Why don't we all go to the carnival on Sunday? That way, Dad can rest tonight.'

The boy wasn't having it. 'No! Everyone else is going tonight! My friends get to go with their parents. Why can't I?'

His mother tried to calm him. 'We could play a game together, just the four of us. What do you think?'

'Monopoly!' The boy's eyes lit up. He ran to get the board game and began setting it up on the coffee table. His father groaned quietly; Monopoly wasn't exactly a quick game.

But Grandpa played along. 'Alright, we'll play, but only for a little while. After dinner, okay?'

As they gathered around the board, the boy declared he'd go first. He rolled the dice and moved his board piece forward. The game was just beginning when the boy landed on Community Chest and drew a card. 'Oh, look! This says everyone has to give me 200 credits,' the boy announced with glee.

'Dad, wake up! I need my 200 credits,' he repeated, as his father fought to stay awake.

'Right, right . . . here's your money,' his father handed over some play cash, barely able to keep his eyes open. Grandma, who had been watching from her chair, chimed in, 'That's enough for tonight. It's getting late, and you have school in the morning.'

The boy protested, but his mother put her foot down. 'No more arguing. You can play on your tablet for 15 minutes, then it's bedtime. Got it?'

The boy reluctantly agreed, as his father was already asleep, snoring softly on the sofa.

The rest of the week passed in a blur of homework, school, and evening routines. Finally, Sunday morning arrived. The boy woke up with a burst of energy. 'It's Sunday! Sunday!' he shouted as he raced through the house. He skidded into the living room, only to find his father in work clothes, shovelling toast into his mouth. The boy's face fell, his earlier enthusiasm evaporating into disappointment. 'But, Dad, you promised! You were supposed to take us to the carnival today. It's the last day! All my friends are going with their parents.'

His father looked apologetic, but firm. 'I'm sorry, son. I have to work. It's the end of the financial year, and we have a big audit tomorrow. I'll make it up to you, I promise.'

The boy's voice wavered as he tried to hold back tears. 'But I told all my friends we'd be there . . . with you. I wanted Grandpa to take pictures of us on the bumper cars.'

The father sighed, feeling the weight of his son's disappointment. He knelt and whispered, 'Please, try to understand. I really can't miss work today.'

The boy's face scrunched up in concentration, and then he asked, 'How much do they pay you?' His father, taken aback, replied, 'I earn around 2000 rupees an hour. But why do you ask?'

Without another word, the boy ran up to his room. Moments later, a loud crash echoed through the house—a sound of shattering crockery. His father jumped up, alarmed. The boy reappeared, hands full of crumpled notes and loose change. He dumped it all on the table in front of his father. 'Here,' he said, tears streaming down his cheeks. 'Will this be enough? Can you stay home now?'

The room fell silent as the father stood there, speechless, his heart breaking. It wasn't just about the money; it was about a promise broken and a little boy's simple wish for time with his dad.

It's a common struggle that resonates with many parents and children. As adults, we often work hard to provide the best for our families, just as our parents did for us. However, while our parents' sacrifices may have given us a better life, they sometimes came at the cost of quality time and shared memories. These memories are irreplaceable and often shape the bond between parent and child. The father in this incident works tirelessly to support his family, but in the process, he misses out on crucial moments with his son. The boy's innocent plea to spend time together reflects a universal truth: children don't measure love in money or gifts but in moments and attention.

As adults, we can often find ourselves in a similar situation. We're caught in the grind of work, focusing on providing a stable life for our children. Yet, we sometimes miss the bigger picture—our kids want our time and presence, not just the benefits our hard work brings. When we plan for the future, do we take time to think about the kind of environment and culture we want to cultivate in our homes? Have we truly reflected on our roles as parents, partners, sons, daughters, or siblings? To be a dedicated family member, we need to immerse ourselves in the lives of our loved ones, engage with them on their terms, and ensure we're fully present in the moment.

Dr Jamin Brahmbhatt, a urologist and robotic surgeon living in New Jersey, sees himself as having two key jobs: one as a surgeon and the other as a father to his three daughters. Known as 'Dr B' to his patients, he is highly attuned to their needs, carefully listening, observing, and asking follow-up questions before making a diagnosis. Notably, his impressive customer satisfaction score of 4.8/5.0 isn't just due to his surgical expertise or successful patient outcomes. It's mainly because patients appreciate how he's a 'good listener' who 'takes time to hear concerns'. Despite his years of experience, Dr B emphasizes the importance of building a relationship based on mutual trust and respect by allowing patients to express themselves fully.

In his 'second job' as a father, Dr B tries not to bring work-related stress home. However, his three daughters often feel that even when he's physically present, his mind is elsewhere. Whether they're talking about school events or weekend plans, they sense that he's not completely listening. Like many working parents, he finds it hard to leave work at the office, as pending tasks and work stressors can still occupy his thoughts. Even the best communicators struggle to maintain the energy needed to be fully engaged with family in the evenings.

Although his daughters are young, they've developed an intuitive understanding of when their father's mind is preoccupied. Appreciating his genuine efforts and limitations, they often take the lead in conversations, encouraging him to open up and share his feelings. Children may seem too young to grasp the complexities of adult life, but they are certainly observant and caring. When they see parents making a genuine effort to connect with them, they are encouraged to respond in kind by demonstrating patience and engaging in meaningful interactions.

Even in his later years, I often saw how Pramukh Swami Maharaj valued his connections with young people. Once, a child approached him and asked, 'Swami, I saw you remove your teeth after lunch yesterday. I tried really hard at home, but mine wouldn't come out . . . when will my teeth come out?' Swamiji responded with a warm laugh, saying, 'Don't try that! When you get to my age, maybe yours will come out too!'

He then took a few minutes to help the child understand dentures, even showing him how he put them in and cares for them. The child's eyes lit up with wonder and curiosity as he discovered something new. Everyone who witnessed the interaction was impressed by how Pramukh Swami Maharaj took the time to engage with the boy, treating him with the warmth of a grandfather. His attentiveness, empathy, and encouragement kept the younger generation connected and eager to learn.

Mahant Swami Maharaj encourages parents to prioritize quality time with family, stressing the importance of routines and rituals, creating platforms for connection, and seeking out opportunities to strengthen bonds. These practices lay the groundwork for creating enduring memories and fostering a lifetime of love, respect, and trust. Just as we organize our workdays to complete tasks efficiently, we can incorporate simple yet meaningful opportunities to enrich our family lives. Here are a few examples:

1. **Family Meals**:
   Sharing food during mealtimes is a simple yet powerful way for families to connect. Whether it's breakfast, lunch, or dinner, gathering around the table fosters communication and creates a sense of belonging. It provides an opportunity for meaningful conversations, allowing everyone to share their thoughts and stories. To make the most of this time, set aside electronic devices and focus on each other.

2. **Shared Hobbies**:
   Embarking on a shared hobby or project can bring families closer through collaboration and mutual

support. It might be something as simple as gardening or as ambitious as building a DIY project or learning a new skill. Even everyday chores can be turned into family activities—cooking, cleaning, and doing laundry together teach useful skills, encourage teamwork, and promote a sense of shared responsibility.

3. **Bedtime Story Routine**:
Creating a bedtime story routine is a wonderful way to bond with children. It's not just about enjoying a good story; it's about nurturing their imagination, instilling values, and forming lasting memories. Telling moral stories from ancient epics such as the Ramayan and Mahabharat, or using educational magazines like the Swaminarayan Bal Prakash, provide valuable life lessons and cultural insights.

4. **Plan Family Trips**:
Family trips are a fantastic way to create shared experiences and explore new places together. Whether it's a weekend picnic, a day at the beach, or a museum visit, these moments away from the daily routine build a treasure trove of memories. Trips don't have to be extravagant for children to enjoy them; what matters most is spending quality time together. To make trips more meaningful, encourage children to participate in the planning process. Create opportunities to learn and take ownership of the experience.

5. **Practicing Faith**:

    Engaging in worship together creates shared moments
    of spirituality and connection. Whether through prayer,
    meditation, yoga, or other rituals, faith not only deepens
    the familial bond but also reinforces shared values and
    beliefs. Pramukh Swami Maharaj advocated for a ghar
    mandir (a sacred space for worship) to be the centrepiece
    of a home. This platform provides a common thread of
    faith and grounding that can guide the family through
    all aspects of life.

PROJECT SYNC

When differences spark conflict, tensions rise, and those closest to us grow distant, the very foundation of our home feels fragile. What we crave is a reliable platform where communication flows freely, understanding deepens, and emotions find expression without fear. Fortunately, such a platform already exists.

In 2003, Shailesh Dhanani, a factory worker from Gujarat, relocated to the city of Rajkot with his newly-wed wife. Though their income was modest, they were fortunate to find a generous landlord who offered them an affordable apartment above his own house. The couple happily embraced their new life and soon welcomed a child into their home. However, as Shailesh's work demands increased, it began to strain their marital harmony. His prolonged working hours led to suspicions from his wife, giving rise to misunderstandings, doubts, and eventually, conflicts. Soon, the sound of long heated arguments became a regular disturbance for the neighbours. The couple didn't want their child growing up in a toxic environment but even as they tried to restrain themselves, the situation only seemed to escalate. Their family, it seemed, was on the brink of collapse.

The breaking point arrived when, during one intense argument, Shailesh's wife declared her intention to end her life. At that critical moment, she rushed out of the house, descending the steps hastily. Sensing her distress, their landlord, Vinod Raiyani, intervened and, upon recognizing her emotional turmoil, inquired about her destination. Overwhelmed and unable to respond, she broke down into tears. Vinod calmly ushered her into his home, where his family was gathered. Joining them, she observed Vinod's family's open engagement, joyful interactions, and spiritual practices. Immersed in the peaceful atmosphere, she gradually felt the weight on her heart begin to lift.

In the following days, Vinod took the initiative to guide Shailesh and his wife. He introduced the couple to his family meetings, an activity termed 'ghar sabha'. Witnessing the positive outcomes, Shailesh initiated these meetings within his own family. Reflecting on the transformation, Shailesh now tells me, 'In the beginning, I used to do ghar sabha on my own. But gradually, all the members joined me. Slowly, my wife too became interested in it. Our differences started to dissolve, and our problems were solved. Finally, there was peace and joy between us.' Today, more than twenty years later, Shailesh and his wife live happily with their parents and children. The credit, they say, belongs to ghar sabha.

'Ghar sabha' or 'family gathering', emerged as a visionary initiative introduced by Pramukh Swami Maharaj. Drawing from decades of experience in diagnosing family conflicts and counselling solutions, Swamiji devised a structured framework to foster constructive dialogue within households. Directly confronting the issue of diminished family engagement, he conceptualized a unique forum where family members could convene regularly, openly express themselves, strengthen their bonds, and share wisdom. Peace and harmony, he would explain, flourish in an environment of love, mutual understanding, acceptance, support, and faith. He believed a peaceful world begins with peaceful homes.

So, how does one conduct a ghar sabha? It starts with all members of the household agreeing on a fixed time to meet, ideally daily or at least two to three times a week. From there, the family follows four integral steps:

1. **Prayer**:
   Begin by setting aside phones, devices, and distractions, and gather in a comfortable and conducive environment. It's recommended to designate a sacred setting within the home, perhaps as a 'ghar-mandir' or shrine. The meeting commences with a prayer for peace, prosperity, and progress, along with a commitment to foster greater family unity.

2. **Learning and Reflecting**:
   As a family, explore profound teachings from good books, sacred texts, or spiritual talks. Reading, reflecting,

and discussing wise words serve as catalysts for positivity and personal growth. Consider incorporating children's publications, like the Swaminarayan Bal Prakash, to empower parents to holistically prepare their children, share their cultural heritage, and teach values such as honesty, respect, and gratitude.

3. **Facilitating Constructive Conversation**:
    Encourage everyone to share recent updates about their lives and collectively plan for the future. Ask questions like, 'How are you feeling?', 'How can I help?', 'What can we do better?', and 'How can we improve our communication?' Let children lead discussions and consider their ambitions. Create a safe space where everyone can regularly and openly express themselves, seek advice, and provide feedback.

4. **Fun and Bonding**:
    Laughter is a powerful tool for relieving tension and breaking down communication barriers. Therefore, integrating team games and shared enjoyment becomes essential for creating deeper connections and lasting memories.

Expanding upon this framework, today, hundreds of thousands of families are empowered through the ghar sabha initiative. Pankaj Patel, an IT Engineer from New Jersey, USA, shares his experience of using ghar sabha as a platform for self-improvement:

Due to my furious nature, I used to get mad at my children for small things. As a result, my wife became averse to me, and my parents didn't like my edgy nature either. But ghar sabha did the trick. We read the BAPS publication, "Swabhav Vash Sansar". It depicts how our innate nature plays havoc in life. Slowly, we became tolerant and broad-minded and . . . started understanding each other's virtues and realized that each one of us was right in his or her own way. We thus came closer to each other and our bitterness vanished.[*]

We prepare a chart in which everyone writes things he or she liked or did not like about the house or its members. We then make clarifications. This has brought us closer. For example, I liked to read while eating, but the children wanted me to speak to them and enjoy; so I changed the habit.

Diptesh Patel, from New Jersey, USA, utilized ghar sabha as a tool to holistically and culturally educate his children. He explains, 'Children are generally easily distracted. My son was interested in video games. But in ghar sabha, we would explain what this meant. Now he realizes that it is not good. We cover different subjects in ghar sabha such as education, health, general knowledge, satsang-based games and others. Thanks to it, my son has become cultured and understands our philosophy.'[†]

---

[*] Swaminarayan Bliss. September–October 2018.
[†] Ibid.

Diptesh elaborates on how he and his wife used ghar sabha to improve their relationship with his parents:

> My retired parents live with me. Often, one finds gaps and bitterness in relationships between mother-in-law and daughter-in-law, and between son and father. The case between my parents and us was similar. My parents were adamant about certain things, whereas my wife and I thought differently. My parents insisted that we raise our children the way they had raised us. But in America, our situation was completely different. Additionally, there were small communication gaps between us and them. For example, I never informed them that I had planned to visit my friend's home the following day. On the other hand, my parents had planned something else for all of us. My wife would often cook something and my mother wished to eat something else. Gradually, through ghar sabha, we were able to solve our problems due to a lack of communication. After completing the ghar sabha, we would discuss our schedules for the next two or three days and what meals to cook. Subsequently, the problems between my mother and wife as well as my father and myself were defused.*

Janak Patel from Surat, India, observed how his eleven-year-old son used ghar sabha as a means to reconnect with his parents: 'He was really hard to talk to. I knew he was

---

* Swaminarayan Bliss. September–October 2018.

hanging out with people his age who were pulling him further away from our family and closer to things I didn't want my son around. One day he came home and said he wanted to start doing ghar sabha. What I realized was that he wanted to talk to me about it all along; he just didn't know how to. Today, we openly discuss his plans for the day, night, and even who he is spending time with. I feel like I didn't know my son until I started doing ghar sabha.'*

Despite the obvious benefits, initiating a shift in one's family culture can be daunting. Addressing this apprehension, Mahant Swami Maharaj provides reassurance, stating, 'In the beginning, you may not get success [in doing ghar sabha], but, gradually, you'll get the hang of it. When one [person in the family] understands, then the second person will also understand and then everyone will understand. The positive effects of [ghar sabha] will gradually become apparent and then solidify. It takes time for everyone in the family to adjust to each other, and then peace and happiness will prevail. Today, countless families experience such peace. If you want to experience the miracle of ghar sabha, then start doing it.'†

---

* Ghar sabha. *BAPS*, https://tinyurl.com/zvjtdyvwx (accessed 11 November 2024).
† Swaminarayan Bliss. September–October 2018.

WHAT MARK
WILL YOU LEAVE?

Have you ever considered what shapes the destiny of our children? Is it fate, family upbringing, the schools they attend, the opportunities they encounter, or perhaps their innate talents and abilities? As we invest considerable time, energy, and resources into nurturing the younger generation, there's a crucial aspect we often overlook: a factor that fundamentally shapes their trajectory.

Once upon a time, in a quiet village, there lived a simple farmer who craved the taste of sweet mangoes. With this longing in his heart, he planted seeds hoping they would yield the fruits of his dreams. Day after day, he tended to the saplings with gentle care, providing just the right amount of water, sunlight, and protection. When they were frail, he sheltered them. When they fell ill, he nursed them back to health. Fifteen years drifted by in quiet anticipation as he watched them grow tall and strong.

However, as the fifteenth summer arrived, his dreams soured into frustration. Each day, he sought the shade of the trees, yearning for the refreshing taste of mangoes. Yet, to his dismay, the fruits dangling from the thorny branches were chewy and bitter. Every day he wondered why his trees would not give mangoes. One day, during a visit to the farm, a friend questioned the farmer's strange behaviour, and it wasn't long until he discovered the mistake. 'You planted the wrong seeds, fool!' He told the farmer, 'These are not mango trees, you must have planted the seed of the thorny Baval trees.' Embarrassed and disappointed, the foolish farmer realized his mistake. He had poured his time, energy, and resources into nurturing trees. But he had carelessly planted the wrong seeds in the first place.

Of course, no farmer I know is likely to make such a big mistake. But the story rings with an insightful lesson. In the world today, we strive to nurture the next generation, pouring our time, energy, and resources into shaping their future. But what seeds are we sowing into their lives? And what fruits do we expect to harvest?

Born into the esteemed Singhania family, Vijaypat joined the family textile business, with its roots dating back to 1925. With Vijaypat as the managing director, Raymond Group earned recognition as one of the most respected clothing brands in the country—a brand synonymous with fine clothing for millions of Indians, staying true to their famous tagline of 'The Complete Man'. His dedication and hard work of over 35 years played a pivotal role in expanding Raymond's portfolio and diversifying its offerings, ensuring its position as a market leader. Beyond his business acumen, Vijaypat received prestigious honours, awards, and global recognition for breaking world records as an aviator and for numerous remarkable achievements.[*] This combination of business success and adventurous spirit cemented his legacy as a pioneering figure.

However, everything changed in 2015 when Vijaypat decided to pass his entire stake in Raymond to his younger son. This decision allegedly set in motion a series of unfortunate events that culminated in the loss of his wealth, life's work, and cherished family home. It reportedly began with a family dispute over property and business. Two years later, at the age of 79, Vijaypat was forced to leave his family home. Despite his remarkable achievements, his later years have been overshadowed by legal battles, strained relationships, and a profound sense of loss and regret.[†]

In his autobiography *An Incomplete Life*, Vijaypat shares a rare glimpse into his journey filled with adventures and undertakings, yet haunted by the painful sting of regret and heartbreak. Summarizing his journey, he explains, 'If only I knew then what I know now, my life would be

---

[*] 26 November 2005. 'Highest Flight by a Hot Air Balloon'. *Guinness World Records*. https://tinyurl.com/nnzubf4kn (accessed 11 November 2024).

[†] Baghel, S. 14 August 2017. '"I was blinded by love for son,' says Vijaypat Singhania'. *Mumbai Mirror*, https://tinyurl.com/3t5rc5kj (accessed 11 November 2024).

completely different.'* More than 'the betrayal', the deep sorrow of being denied the opportunity to spend time with his beloved grandchildren pains him the most. Reflecting on his journey brings us back to the critical question: after tending and toiling day and night for his children, what kind of fruit did he receive in return?

Parents invest nearly everything for the sake of their children. They purchase a family home to provide ample space for their children to live and grow. They spend nights soothing a crying child to sleep and days making silly faces just to see them smile. They work tirelessly across decades to provide food, gifts, and a decent education. They even squeeze out the remaining time to drive them to music classes, sports activities, and friends' birthdays. Yet, despite these remarkable investments, we often overlook a critical need—instilling values.

In our modern education system, the primary focus is on producing highly skilled and proficient workers across various fields and disciplines. Unfortunately, there's not enough emphasis on nurturing values from an early age. This gap in the curriculum is evident. While we rightly prioritize STEAM subjects (Science, Technology, Engineering, Arts, and Mathematics), the essential focus on fostering compassion, resilience, and moral awareness in children is often lacking.

---

* Singhania, Vijaypat. 31 October 2021. *An Incomplete Life: The Autobiography* Hardcover.

Elaborating on this during a teachers' conference in 2003, Pramukh Swami Maharaj explained, 'Valueless education destroys, whereas value-based education protects. We acquire knowledge through education, but the essence of life lies in values such as morality, honesty, compassion, forgiveness, tolerance, being helpful to others, recognizing the good in others' deeds, and contributing to the upliftment of our country and society.' With this in mind, Swamiji often warned parents, stating, 'If you fail to instill values in your children, you risk losing both your children and your wealth.'

In the 17th century, Chhatrapati Shivaji Maharaj emerged as a wise and just ruler of India. He dedicated himself to protecting the weak, fostering employment opportunities for people of all faiths and castes, advocating for the respectful treatment of women, and ushering in a golden age of prosperity through his Maratha empire.* Shivaji's enduring legacy is evident in the ongoing celebration of his life and the numerous statues erected in his honour across India. The foundation of his success can be traced back to his childhood. Alongside receiving a comprehensive education, his mother, Jijabai, imparted moral lessons drawn from heroic figures such as Bhagwan Shri Rama, Bhagwan Shri Krishna, and Yudhishthir found in the sacred texts of the Ramayan and Mahabharat. She

---

* Sarkar, Jadunath. 1920. 'Shivaji and His Times'. *University of California Libraries*, London, New York, Longmans, Green and co. pp. 20–30, 43, 437, 158, 163.

used these role models to instil values of responsibility, honour, integrity, compassion, and courage.

Upon being crowned king of the Maratha Empire, Shivaji's first act was not to address the nearly 50,000 admirers at the ceremony but to bow before his mother and touch her feet.* He remained grounded, unaffected by fame and power. When Jijabai had planted seeds of values in her child's heart, she didn't just create a powerful king; perhaps more profoundly, she nurtured a mature, respectful, and humble human being. According to Hindu tradition, a mother who imparts values to her children deserves the honour equivalent to a million teachers. Such parents carefully sculpt the character of their children, serving as the unsung heroes behind the rise of great personalities throughout the ages.

Pramukh Swami Maharaj was a passionate advocate for childcare. On 10 November 2006, he shared his practical wisdom on effective upbringing during the Parents' Day event in London. He emphasized, 'Due to work, business, or other activities, we fail to spend sufficient time sitting with our children, and when the children are deprived of love, care and attention, they turn more and more towards watching television and other such things. To be a parent means to love unconditionally, to provide them warmth, and to be there for them. If you can foster a deep and affectionate bond of love for each other, then, even if the

---

* Ibid.

child's behaviour is challenging, they will gently improve over time.'

But of course, Pramukh Swami Maharaj also recognized the intricate challenges parents encounter in nurturing their children amid the demands of modern life. With financial pressures, time constraints, and the complexities of contemporary parenting, ensuring children receive the best values can seem daunting. However, even amid these challenges, parents can prioritize quality over quantity. Spending dedicated, meaningful time with their children, even if limited, can have a profound impact.

This could involve engaging in open and honest conversations, participating in shared activities, and leading by example. Additionally, seeking support from family, community, or spiritual leaders can provide guidance and strength in navigating these challenges. By embodying the values they wish to instil in their children and by fostering a nurturing and supportive environment at home, parents can indeed become positive role models, laying a strong foundation for their children's growth and development.

To support parents in nurturing their children, Yogiji Maharaj formally established the BAPS Children's Forum in 1954. Over the years, Pramukh Swami Maharaj and Mahant Swami Maharaj expanded these activities worldwide. Today, with the support of core 20,000 BAPS volunteers, over 150,000 children are guided annually across 40 countries to lead moral lives and serve society.* The vision goes

---

* 'Children's Day: Celebrating the Future'. *PSM100*, https://tinyurl.com/ y674dr36 (accessed 11 November 2024).

beyond producing engineers, doctors, and pilots; it aims to cultivate good human beings. Children are inspired to embody the values of respect, honesty, spirituality, and moral responsibility.

In the upcoming chapters, we will explore simple tools and activities that families can utilize to ensure their children receive the value-based upbringing they need. By sharing expertise in these areas, parents are empowered to become better role models and positively influence the younger generation. As the old proverb goes, 'A child's life is like a piece of paper on which every person leaves a mark.' The question then arises: What mark will you leave?

THE GENERATION GAP

Frequently, parents may unknowingly impose their ideas and worldviews onto their children, neglecting to truly understand their emotions. Consequently, this can lead to a widening gap between parents and children, creating a sense of distance. However, it is possible to bridge these boundaries if we take the time to learn how.

In a typical home, it is a familiar sight to find a teenager fully absorbed in their smartphone, whether engrossed in chats with friends, browsing social media, or indulging in games. Recognizing the concerns surrounding excessive screen time, parents feel compelled to intervene. With genuine intentions, they may decide to confiscate the teenager's smartphone and impose restrictions on its usage.

Unfortunately, the sudden decision often leaves the teenager feeling distraught and resentful. Overwhelmed by these emotions, they begin to withdraw from their parents, seeking solace in secrecy. Their room becomes a fortress, locked and impenetrable, and conversations become scarce, if not non-existent. The growing divide in communication intensifies as the teenager believes their parents are incapable of truly understanding them. Regrettably, this disconnect continues to widen as time goes on.

In such situations, the parents intend to guide and protect their children. However, the way their concern was addressed led to unintended consequences. Reflecting on their broken relationship, such parents often wonder, 'Where did we go wrong?'

It's a striking irony of the 21st century that young individuals often find solace in sharing their lives with friends, and at times even strangers they've met through social media, yet they struggle to openly communicate their emotions and thoughts with the very people who brought them into this world. The rapid pace of cultural shifts and the widespread adoption of technology have contributed to the emergence of a significant generation gap. In light of these circumstances, there is an urgent need for both parents and children to make concerted efforts to genuinely understand and connect.

On his return from America, Sardar Vallabhbhai Patel's grandson, Bipin, expressed a desire to meet his grandfather. His father, Dahyabhai, agreed but upon noticing Bipin's clothes, he advised, 'Son, if you go to meet him in these clothes made in a mill, how will he feel? Because he firmly insists on wearing the khadi attire.'

Of course, Bipin was fully aware that his grandfather was a prominent leader of the Indian independence movement and an advocate of the khadi ideology. He emphasized the importance of wearing khadi clothes, a hand-spun and hand-woven fabric, as a symbol of self-reliance and resistance against foreign exploitation. Despite knowing this, Bipin didn't feel the need to wear a khadi; he felt comfortable wearing his modern attire.

Before meeting Sardar, Bipin's aunt, Maniben, also warned Bipin, 'If you go in these clothes to meet your grandpa, he will scold you.' But Bipin turned a deaf ear to her words too.

Upon entering the room, Sardar's keen eyesight took note of Bipin's modern attire immediately. Bipin started to feel a little nervous and Maniben too felt that Sardar would express his displeasure. But to their surprise, Sardar did not say anything. Then, Maniben herself decided to raise the issue, 'Bapu, look at the clothes this kid is wearing. I told him to wear a khadi. What if someone were to see him here and ask you why your own grandson is not wearing khadi while you keep insisting on everyone wearing it?'

Sardar calmly replied, 'Bipin is not a small kid anymore that we have to explain things to him. If he does not believe in it, let him not wear a khadi. What's the big deal? Wearing a khadi without believing in it will not reap any benefit.'

Bipin was thrilled that his grandfather could respect and understand his point of view. Here, Sardar's action underscores the importance of embracing the perspectives and choices of the younger generation, recognizing that their individuality and beliefs may differ from traditional expectations. It emphasizes the need to foster an environment of acceptance and respect, acknowledging that true understanding goes beyond superficial judgements and extends to appreciating the evolving values and preferences of the modern world.

There are moments, however, when it becomes imperative for a parent to fulfil their duty by intervening or guiding their child. Failing to provide the necessary guidance may lead to negative consequences. Yet, the challenge lies in striking the delicate balance between fulfilling parental responsibilities and avoiding actions that may push the child further away. How, then, can parents navigate this complex terrain, ensuring they do what is right for their child while maintaining a healthy connection?

In 1992, a group of American youths embarked on a journey to immerse themselves in Indian culture. As their visit drew to a close, they seized the opportunity to meet Pramukh Swami Maharaj in Ahmedabad. One of the elders noticed that one of the youths was wearing earrings and, believing it to be an appropriate occasion, decided to bring this matter to Swamiji's attention with the hope that he would advise against wearing them.

'Swami, can such earrings be worn?' the elder asked.

Empathizing with the youth, Swamiji replied, 'What's wrong with it? It may seem new to you, but in our days, many of the affluent men of the Charotar region and other places wore earrings.'

Surprised by the response, the elder tried to clarify Swamiji's guidance, 'So you want him to continue wearing them?'

Swamiji then expressed his wish in a gentle tone. There was no insistence in his words but there was clarity. Listening to Swamiji's personal preference for him to give up the earrings, the youth happily took his advice.

By cultivating an environment characterized by acceptance, respecting individual independence, and acknowledging emotions, we can effectively bridge the boundaries that often create family divisions. It is essential to approach guidance with sensitivity, allowing younger members to make their own choices while gently guiding them along the way. In doing so, we can foster deeper connections and cultivate lasting affection within our families, nurturing a sense of unity and understanding that withstands the test of time.

PARENTING IN THE DIGITAL WORLD

Cyberbullying, diminishing attention spans, mental health issues, and screen addiction—these are not merely challenges for adults, but also daily experiences for toddlers and teens. While technology has provided convenience, it has also harshly exposed the new generation to harmful content and habits. The issue is escalating, and there's only one challenging path forward: parents must translate their concerns into concrete action.

Imagine your typical toddler, just beginning to walk and stumbling over furniture as he tries. Yet, no number of stumbles will deter him from his goal. Amidst the locks of his curly hair, he spots his dad's phone resting on the sofa as his father watches TV. He rushes to the sofa, grabs the phone, and manages to press the right buttons to start his favourite online show. Despite his fingers occasionally missing the mark, after a few attempts, he succeeds and becomes engrossed in the screen. His father knows it's best to let him watch because any attempt to take away the phone will result in a screaming match with his three-year-old.

Anyone reading this, whether as a parent, sibling, or relative, likely recognizes a child like the one described. This scenario underscores a concerning trend: the increasing integration of children and technology. While we often hear about the dangers of allowing children to use technology, we cannot overlook its benefits. Social media enables children to connect with family members across the globe, and modern educational games facilitate language development and learning. Additionally, technology serves as a convenient tool—for children, it offers quick and guaranteed entertainment, while for parents, it provides some peace and quiet as the child is occupied. Furthermore, technology seems tailored to captivate a child's attention with its vibrant colours, targeted content in shows, and engaging games.

For parents, exercising caution is essential. Typically, parents meticulously inspect anything they give to their child—almost instinctively. Some items are easily identified as potentially hazardous, such as plug sockets, fire, and cigarettes. However, certain items entail a necessary risk and demand closer attention. Take a knife, for instance. Initially, parents refrain from allowing their young children near sharp objects, recognizing the inherent danger. Nevertheless, they realize that eventually their child must learn to use a knife. Therefore, they introduce supervised access at an appropriate age, starting with a blunt knife and teaching safe handling while remaining mindful of the risks. Parents grant more freedom with time, but only when they are confident in their children's abilities.

Likewise, in the realm of technology, parents must educate themselves about its potential dangers and take proactive steps to train their children accordingly. Just as a child progresses from supervised handling of a blunt knife to safely using a sharp one independently, parents must oversee their children's technological journey, ensuring they develop the necessary awareness and skills to navigate the digital world safely. Parental guidance and supervision are crucial in shaping children's interactions with technology, empowering them to make informed decisions and cultivate responsible digital citizenship.

Firstly, parents must acknowledge their role in guiding their children's discernment, especially considering their limited judgement at a young age. When a shiny object is placed in front of a young child, their instinct is to reach for it. While this innate curiosity fosters creativity and motor skills, parents intervene to determine what is beneficial for their child's development. Mahant Swami Maharaj often emphasizes the significance of parents actively exercising discernment in their children's lives. He highlights how, unlike in traditional societies, parents today bear a greater responsibility. In the past, communities often lived together, with extended family members playing significant roles in children's upbringing. Children frequently attended gurukuls (traditional Indian residential schools) where wise gurus imparted values such as discernment, self-discipline, and responsibility. Parents relied on the support of their community, as the saying goes, 'it takes a village' to raise a child.

However, with the rise of nuclear families, the burden of children's upbringing often falls solely on parents. It has never been more crucial for parents to comprehend the world in which their children are growing up and the associated dangers. Recognizing this, the importance of establishing strict guidelines while providing a well-rounded upbringing cannot be overstated.

As parents, we often attempt to shield our children from negative exposure, but are we truly delving into the issue to the extent required? A report in the *Times of India* in 2023 revealed that 42 per cent of children under the age of twelve in India spend up to four hours a day glued to screens.[*] Many parents I've spoken to express a common struggle: the constant battle when asking children to put down tablets, smartphones, or game consoles. Recent studies in the US have underscored this concern: in 2016, 10.3 per cent of students reported staying home from school due to cyberbullying. By 2023, that number nearly doubled to 19.2 per cent.[†] These studies emphasize that surface-

---

[*] 2023. '42% of children below age of 12 spend up to 4 hours daily glued to screens'. *Times of India*, https://tinyurl.com/3ffbdby5 (accessed 3 March 2024).

[†] Patchin, J.W. 'Cyberbullying continues to rise among youth in the United States'. *Cyberbullying Research Centre*. https://tinyurl.com/3d3uxavu (accessed 3 March 2024).

level screening is insufficient; parents must invest the time to genuinely understand what constitutes the best use of technology for their child.

Setting boundaries is crucial, but we must go further. Children learn by observing the actions of those around them, especially their parents. Therefore, if parents aim to instil healthy screen habits in their children, they must first demonstrate those habits themselves. Picture a scenario where a child refuses to eat a particular food. Instead of simply insisting, the parent takes a bite themselves. This simple act often encourages the child to try the food. Similarly, parents can apply this principle to screen time. By being mindful of their own screen usage in front of their children, parents create an environment where healthy screen habits are modelled and normalized. Children naturally look up to their parents, mimicking their behaviour in various aspects of life. Therefore, if parents consistently prioritize screen-free activities and limit their own screen time, children are more likely to follow suit. Just as parents lead by example in promoting physical health through exercise and nutritious eating, they must also model healthy digital habits.

Dhaval Mistry, a volunteer with BAPS UK and Europe's parenting and children support, shares a personal journey that many new parents might find familiar. As he and his wife prepared for parenthood, they became increasingly observant of the interactions between parents and their children in everyday settings such as supermarkets, playgrounds, libraries, and even bus stops. One striking observation was the widespread captivation of babies and toddlers with digital screens, from the glow of smartphones to the flicker of tablets. In their quest to navigate these modern parental challenges, Dhaval and his wife sought wisdom in the enlightening words of Mahant Swami Maharaj. His frequently echoed analogy, 'The contents of the bucket come from the well,' deeply inspired them, emphasizing the critical responsibility of parents to lead by example.

As Dhaval and his wife awaited the arrival of their child, they became keenly aware of how their screen habits might impact their newborn. This realization prompted a significant lifestyle change. They actively reduced their screen time, cut out movies and TV shows, and sought screen-free methods for completing daily tasks whenever possible. This adjustment freed up time for enriching experiences with their son, Neelkanth. They explored the joys of reading and museum visits, and embraced language learning through interaction. They also ignited creativity with music, storytelling, dance, and a variety of games, fostering both indoor and outdoor play.

This transformative approach has become prevalent in the BAPS community, with families like those of Samarth and Moksh from Milton Keynes adopting similar principles. Samarth's parents incorporated screen-free activities into their daily lives, encouraging creativity, reading and active engagement, while Moksh's parents focused on nurturing personal interactions and cultural discovery.

When it comes to screen time activities, especially with young children, parents can actively participate alongside them. If a child expresses interest in watching something, parents can suggest informative content such as documentaries and watch together. They can then discuss the documentary together to create shared learning experiences. This not only promotes quality bonding time, but also provides parents with insight into the content their child is consuming. Engaging with children during screen time fosters transparency and openness in the parent-child relationship. When children see their parents actively involved in their digital experiences from a young age, they will feel more comfortable sharing their thoughts and concerns as they grow older.

In essence, navigating the journey of parenting in the digital age requires a delicate balance between embracing the benefits of technology and safeguarding against its potential pitfalls. Much like guiding a child's journey with a knife, from supervised use to independent mastery, parents must approach technology with a similar mindset of gradual exposure and discernment. Through leading by example, creating a safe environment, and offering patient guidance, parents possess the capability to empower their children in this constantly evolving digital era.

AGE OF HONOUR

As the world's population ages at an unprecedented rate, the challenges and implications of this demographic shift burden healthcare systems and policymakers. However, it's not just a challenge for governments—it's a deeply personal issue that affects us all. As we navigate the reality of having ageing family members and contemplate our own ageing process, we must reconsider our role in this evolving landscape. Let's start with a case study.

Akshay stood before the mirror, carefully perfecting his hairstyle, the final touch to his impeccable appearance. Today held a significant event for him—the international youth conference where he would address the audience on the topic of respect. As he adjusted his tie, his mind echoed with the pride of being a role model, exemplified by his selfless care for his elderly mother.

'I have such a big heart,' he thought, 'I could have put Mom in a care home, but I took the noble decision of letting her live with us instead.' Straightening his tie, Akshay marvelled at his own brilliance.

'Akshay dear,' came Amma's voice from across the hall. Checking the time, Akshay couldn't afford to delay. The conference awaited, and a multitude of eager faces anticipated his words. Despite the urgency, he approached his mother's room, acknowledging her needs.

Amma, her frail frame bearing the weight of severe arthritis, reached out for the pain balm once more, silently beseeching Akshay for relief. However, the impending conference loomed over him, and the thought of arriving late with the lingering scent of balm on his hands ignited frustration. In a moment of exasperation, Akshay raised his voice and unleashed a torrent of grievances. He berated Amma for her disregard for his time, her relentless demands, and the inconveniences she caused.

Amma's wrinkled face barely moved. She didn't say a word. What was there to say?

Amid this tension, Akshay's twelve-year-old son, Amar, appeared. He was bewildered by the commotion. Akshay, seeking an ally, vented about Grandma's alleged unreasonableness. Amar listened carefully and lent support to his father's grievances. Then, with a deep breath, Akshay headed towards the door. Yet, just as he thought he could escape the turmoil, Amar, inquisitive about his father's speech, asked the crucial question, 'Hey Dad, what's the topic for your speech today?'

'Respect,' Akshay replied with a smile. However, the words echoed back to him, revealing a stark truth. The smile faded, and a realization hit him—he was a hypocrite, preaching respect while failing to embody it at that very moment. Caught in his internal struggle, Akshay's son stepped forward, placing a gentle hand on his shoulder. Amar reassured, 'Don't worry, Dad. I'll look after Amma. You go to the conference.'

At that moment, Akshay understood the true essence of respect—the sacrifice it demanded and its profound significance. Amar's understanding and compassion spoke volumes, and with newfound clarity, Akshay acknowledged, 'We both will take care of her.' As Akshay applied pain balm to Amma's aching joints, the conference audience awaited his speech on respect, unaware of the important lesson he had just learned—that respect is not just spoken, but lived through patience, compassion, and sacrifice.

The prospect of ageing is not eagerly anticipated, yet it is an inevitable part of the human journey. Indeed, the ageing process can be unforgiving, marked by the gradual erosion of youthful vitality and the emergence of physical and emotional challenges. As years pass, bodies weaken, skin loses its elasticity, and senses begin to falter. Yet, perhaps the most profound aspect of ageing is the shift in perspective it brings. Those who have spent a lifetime devoted to their families may find themselves grappling with the newfound need for care and support, a realization that can be both humbling and heart-wrenching.

In the eyes of youth, the elderly may seem slow and out of touch, their experiences dismissed as irrelevant. However, what the young often fail to appreciate is that with age comes a wealth of wisdom borne from life's trials and tribulations. Roman Philosopher Cicero explains, 'There is assuredly nothing dearer to a man than wisdom, and though age takes away all else, it undoubtedly brings us that.' The ups and downs of existence serve as the most potent teacher, imparting lessons that can only be learned through the passage of time.

In families where multiple generations coexist, the treatment of elders serves as a powerful example for impressionable young minds. Children observe how their parents honour and respect their grandparents, internalizing these behaviours and carrying them forward into their own lives. For Amar, witnessing his father's transformative realization served as a poignant lesson in the importance of respecting one's elders. It was a defining moment that will shape how Amar will treat Akshay in the coming decades. Ultimately, the respect we maintain for our elders serves as a testament to the values we hold dear and the legacy we hope to leave behind. It is the pledge to uphold the bonds of family and community that ensures future generations continue to cherish and honour the wisdom of their predecessors.

Rooted in the teachings of the sacred text Taittiriya Upanishad, the Hindu mantra embodies the sentiment of reverence towards parents: 'Matru devo bhava, Pitru devo bhava'—encouraging us to regard our mother and father as divine beings deserving of the highest respect. It is considered one of the noblest responsibilities of sons and daughters to care for their parents in their old age because it carries the honour of acknowledging the selfless sacrifices they have made.

Mahant Swami Maharaj advocates the timeless practice of bowing to one's parents every morning and seeking their blessings. This practice, he emphasizes, should not wane with age but continue into adulthood, serving as a tangible expression of gratitude for the unwavering love and guidance received throughout life. The duty to care for our parents does not diminish with time but rather intensifies. Just as our parents lovingly nurtured and cared for us in our infancy, it is incumbent upon us to reciprocate that love and care until the very end of their lives. By embodying the principles of selflessness and devotion towards our parents, we honour not only familial bonds, but also uphold the sacred teachings that guide us toward a life of compassion and righteousness.

Guided by the steadfast leadership of Mahant Swami Maharaj, who champions the invaluable role of elders in our community, BAPS Charities orchestrates regular health drives worldwide. These initiatives, conducted in collaboration with other charitable organizations and healthcare providers, aim to raise awareness and screening for prevalent conditions such as cancer, dementia, and cardiovascular disease. Additionally, they offer vital health screenings to individuals in need.[*]

Yet, what truly distinguishes these efforts is the heartfelt initiative to honour and cherish the elderly. Inspired by

---

[*] *BAPS Charities.* https://tinyurl.com/yc436sdj (accessed 11 November 2024).

Mahant Swami Maharaj's teachings, young teens take the lead in spearheading community outreach projects. Volunteers of BAPS Charities UK visited over 40 care homes, nursing homes, and hospital wards across England, seeking meaningful engagement with the elderly. In environments often marked by loneliness and monotony, these interactions breathe new life and joy into the hearts of elderly residents. For many, it is a rare chance to connect with energetic and thoughtful teenagers, offering moments of respite from the solitude of their daily lives. One such resident, Minnie, residing at Kenbrook Care Home, expressed her profound gratitude, declaring, 'This is the most enjoyable experience I've had since my husband passed away 19 years ago. Thank you!'*

While the young volunteers derive satisfaction from bringing happiness to the seniors, they are astounded by the depth of their own personal growth. Through these meaningful encounters, they gain a heightened awareness of the world and its diverse inhabitants, bridging the generation gap with empathy, compassion, and selfless service. In the process, they uncover invaluable life lessons that resonate far beyond the confines of their immediate experiences. These profound experiences are carried back to their homes and classrooms and shared with their fellow youth: 'To serve our elders is not merely a duty,' one female volunteer explained,

---

* 'Care for the Elderly: BAPS Swaminarayan Sanstha's On-going Community Outreach Project'. *BAPS Swaminarayan Sanstha*, https://tinyurl.com/4xv4c6y6 (accessed 11 November 2024).

'But a privilege and sacred opportunity that enriches both giver and receiver alike.'

Sylvia first discovered this sentiment during her visit to the Cultural Festival of India in 1991. It was a 31-day celebration, held on the lawns of Middlesex County College, New Jersey, USA. BAPS hosted this event in America to offer 1.2 million people, like Sylvia, a comprehensive experience of Indian culture, history, and values.

As the local college administrator, Sylvia decided to explore the festival. Her curiosity drew her to the 'Beautiful Borderless World' exhibition. There, she witnessed the portrayal of the child role-model Shravan from the ancient sacred text, the Ramayan. As she listened to the narration of how Shravan fulfilled his elderly parents' last wish to go on a pilgrimage, Sylvia was deeply moved.

'Since Shravan could not afford transport,' the guide explained, 'the boy decided to put each parent in a basket and tie each basket to the ends of a bamboo pole, which he would carry on his shoulder. His parents were blind, yet he never questioned the necessity for them to visit sacred places. Instead, he faithfully carried them long distances, bathing them, feeding them, and serving them.'

To the guide's surprise, Sylvia burst into tears before quickly leaving the exhibition. She headed straight to the local care home where her elderly parents resided. Baffled, her parents watched as she signed their discharge papers, gathered their belongings, and ushered them into her car. 'What's going on, Sylvia?' her mother inquired. 'I am no longer your Sylvia,' she responded, 'I am your Shravan.'

Guiding her parents back to the exhibition, Sylvia emotionally explained to them the story of Shravan, her regrets, and her promise to diligently care for them. Witnessing Sylvia embrace her parents, the guide learned something profound. 'Shravan is not just an ancient story,' he expressed, 'but a timeless message for all sons and daughters to reconnect with their parents. Serving them is not a burden, but our duty, privilege, and honour.'

WORK ETHICS AND HUMAN RELATIONS

VALUES STRONGER THAN STEEL

What sets apart fleeting success from enduring greatness? What distinguishes ordinary achievers from legends? While intelligence, talent, and experience can take us far, the lives of the legends demonstrate certain qualities that create an enduring impact. As we explore what it truly means to lead with values, we equip ourselves with the tools to leave a lasting impression of our own.

Taj Mahal Palace Hotel, Mumbai, India
Wednesday, 26 November 2008
9.38 p.m.

It was an ordinary weekday evening at the Taj Hotel in Mumbai, bustling with close to 500 registered guests and hosting another 500-600 attendees at various functions in its banquet halls and restaurants. Laughter and conversation filled the air as guests enjoyed their parties and dinners. However, the routine atmosphere was about to be shattered. A mere 200 metres from the Taj, an explosion ripped through the Leopold Cafe, sending shockwaves through the crowded streets. Amidst the chaos, two terrorists brandishing automatic weapons began indiscriminate firing.

As panic spread, people sought refuge in the nearby Taj Hotel, only to find themselves facing a new threat. Two heavily armed assailants, armed with grenades and AK-47s, bypassed the hotel's security measures and infiltrated the lobby. While the guests initially mistook the firing as festive firecrackers, the staff members quickly recognized the danger. Reacting swiftly, employees moved to secure the restaurant doors and guide guests to safety, urging them to seek shelter in their rooms. In the heart of the chaos, the Taj Hotel found itself under siege. With the lives of over 1,100 guests hanging in the balance, a battle for survival had begun.

At that critical moment, the majority of the 600 staff members on duty at the Taj Hotel were young, some of whom were parents and the primary breadwinners for their families. They had been trained to memorize the nooks and crannies of the hotel and imprint every back route and exit in their mind. In other words, they all knew how to escape, that too fast. In such situations, one might naturally expect the instinctive response to flee for personal safety or to seek refuge in hiding. However, what unfolded that night was nothing short of extraordinary. Despite the imminent danger, not a single one of the 600 Taj employees abandoned their posts. Their collective actions epitomized heroism in its truest form.

Among the brave souls present on that harrowing day was Mallika Jagad, a 24-year-old banquet manager. Amid the chaos, she retained remarkable composure, taking charge of the event hosting Unilever's top management. With quick thinking, Mallika asked spouses to separate to reduce the risk of losing families and insisted on staying until every person in the hall had been safely evacuated.[*]

Karambir Singh Kang, serving as a General Manager at the Taj Mumbai, was away from the hotel when the attack unfolded. Yet, he swiftly responded to the call of duty by returning to the hotel. Tragically, a fire engulfed his wife and two sons in their living quarters on the sixth floor. Despite this devastating loss, Karambir remained resolute in his commitment to ensuring the safety of others. He continued to lead and guide evacuations, retaining remarkable strength in the face of personal grief. It wasn't until noon the following day that he found the opportunity to inform his parents of the heartbreaking loss his family had endured.[†]

Thomas Varghese, a senior waiter at the hotel's esteemed Wasabi restaurant, emerged as yet another hero during the ordeal. Despite the chaos, his remarkable bravery was evident when he instructed guests to crouch down for

---

[*] '15 years of 26/11: Five heroes who saved hundreds in 2008 Mumbai terror attacks'. *Hindustan Times*, https://tinyurl.com/ydshjem7 (accessed 12 November 2024).

[†] Ibid.

safety before leading them in an orderly evacuation down a staircase. Tragically, Thomas was struck down by gunfire, bravely sacrificing himself as the last person to leave the area.[*]

The Taj Hotel staff all behaved with heroism: many chefs lost their lives while forming a human chain to escort guests out of the kitchen, and the hotel's team of telephone operators called up each guest room to assist and comfort them until 4.30 a.m. All remained calm and composed, prioritizing guests' safety over their own.[†]

Tragically, among the 34 lives lost that day, 17 were those of Taj employees.[‡] Put yourself in their shoes: faced with such terror, isn't it but natural to flee and seek personal safety? So, what compelled them to stay and face danger? What motivated every employee to transcend the ordinary and embrace extraordinary courage?

Harvard Professor Rohit Deshpande delved into this phenomenon and conducted a detailed case study titled 'The Ordinary Heroes of the Taj'.[§] His research uncovered a significant revelation: there were no established protocols or manuals dictating how to respond in such harrowing circumstances. Even individuals at the highest levels of group leadership, including Ratan Tata, were unable to

---

[*] Ibid.

[†] 'The Ordinary Heroes of the Taj'. *Harvard Business Review*, https://tinyurl. com/4nwnrure (accessed 12 November 2024).

[‡] 'The Ordinary Heroes of the Taj Hotel: Rohit Deshpande at TEDxNewEngland'. *YouTube*. https://tinyurl.com/26bnzr5j (accessed 12 November 2024)

[§] 'The Ordinary Heroes of the Taj'. *Harvard Business Review*, https://tinyurl. com/4nwnrure (accessed 12 November 2024).

articulate why these employees exhibited such remarkable behaviour. However, Deshpande's investigation ultimately unveiled a profound insight: the employees' extraordinary response was deeply ingrained in the Taj Group's customer-centric culture. They prioritized values-driven recruitment and placed guests' needs above corporate interests.

Most intriguingly, Deshpande's interactions shed light on the Taj Group's unique approach to talent acquisition. Rather than focusing solely on qualifications or prestigious academic backgrounds, the Taj sought candidates from small towns imbued with traditional Indian values such as reverence for elders, humility, compassion, and honesty. Their recruitment was based not on grades or top-tier colleges but on character, attitude, and values.

Absolutely, it's undeniably true that intelligence, talent, and experience are crucial ingredients for success. But what elevates a person from merely successful to legendary status? Regardless of their background or credentials, it's the values they uphold that truly define and set them apart. In the eyes of hiring managers, integrity, humility, and self-discipline should be prized qualities. These traits signify not only competence but also reliability and ethical behaviour. After all, the legends we truly admire possess unwavering work ethics and a firm commitment to their values.

Consider the case of Sachin Tendulkar, revered as the 'God of Cricket'.* Beyond his unparalleled record-breaking

---

* 'Sachin Tendulkar'. *ESPN*, https://tinyurl.com/2dw4kbsx (accessed 12 November 2024).

feats on the cricket field, Tendulkar was renowned for his unwavering integrity and spirit of collaboration. A striking example of this was witnessed during the 2011 ICC World Cup match between India and West Indies in Chennai. During a pivotal moment in the game, a delivery from Ravi Rampaul grazed the edge of Tendulkar's bat before being caught by the wicketkeeper. Despite the umpire declaring him not out, Tendulkar voluntarily walked off the field. For a player of Tendulkar's stature, competing in what would be his final World Cup, the decision to uphold such honesty amidst intense competition undoubtedly carried immense difficulty. Yet, for Tendulkar, cricket transcended mere victory; it was about upholding the integrity of the sport.

In reaffirming his commitment to principle over personal gain, Tendulkar exemplified not only greatness as a cricketer but also as a true sportsman. Recognizing the weight of his influence as a role model, he embraced a life guided by integrity. This commitment extended far beyond the cricket pitch; Tendulkar staunchly refused to endorse anything that contradicted his deeply held values. Notably, he declined lucrative offers, including blank cheques from tobacco companies, refusing to compromise his principles for financial gain. In doing so, Tendulkar underscored his status not only as a cricketing legend, but also as a beacon of integrity and ethical conduct.[*]

---

[*] "'They offered me a blank cheque . . .' Sachin Tendulkar Revealed a Big Secret Behind Not Advertising For Tobacco Companies.', *Cric Informer*, https://tinyurl.com/2s44y9j8 (accessed 12 November 2024).

Despite being the focal point of attention, Sachin Tendulkar consistently carves out time to support and motivate young players. During the 2023 ICC World Cup, as Virat Kohli showcased his skills on the field, Tendulkar tweeted, 'I hope you [. . .] break my record in the next few days.'* He even shared tips with players from rival teams. Such kindness echoes the sentiments of Mahant Swami Maharaj: 'True greatness lies in those who harbour no envy.' Unlike the cut-throat competition often seen in today's corporate culture, individuals like Tendulkar demonstrate the true essence of finding fulfilment in helping others while still achieving personal success. While Tendulkar's talent and skills brought him achievements, it was his values that secured him a permanent place in the hearts of Indians.

Throughout his life, Pramukh Swami Maharaj emphasized the importance of upholding one's values, regardless of the circumstances. I remember hearing about a remarkable incident that took place in 1977. While staying in Leicester, UK, Pramukh Swami Maharaj encountered a situation concerning the collection of fresh flowers for offering to God. Several children had been assigned the seva of gathering flowers, with neighbours allowing one to two flowers daily from their gardens. Upon discovering that the children were picking three flowers instead of the permitted amount, albeit with the intention of informing the owners later, Pramukh Swami Maharaj immediately summoned them. Addressing the children directly, Swamiji shared a

---

* *X*, https://tinyurl.com/4w8m87vd (accessed 12 November 2024).

teaching from Bhagwan Swaminarayan. He explained that compromising one's honesty, even for a single flower, was not permissible.

Instilling honesty in children shapes them into adults with the utmost integrity. The importance of such teachings becomes evident in challenging moral dilemmas. For instance, Nilesh Patel faced a difficult situation while working at a store in America. As usual, an elderly customer entrusted him to check her lottery ticket while she shopped for groceries. He expected to inform her, once again, of a loss. However, when he scanned the ticket, he realized it was a winner—$300,000!

In a fleeting moment, he recalled his dire financial situation and was tempted to swap the ticket and claim the prize for himself. But, remembering Pramukh Swami Maharaj's teachings, he immediately dismissed the thought. Instead, he duly informed the elderly lady of her lottery win. Though tempted by wealth, his adherence to his values empowered him to uphold his honesty.

The impact of such values extends far beyond those directly involved, leaving a profound impression even on those on the periphery. One notable example took place on 30 September 1988, when Ralph Lamberti, the 12th Borough President of Staten Island, enthusiastically bestowed upon Pramukh Swami Maharaj the honour of 'Key to the Heart'. Intrigued by the president's decision, Viveksagar Swami inquired, 'You have never met Pramukh Swami before today. And you don't know much about his life. Why do you offer such a significant honour to him?'

In response, Lamberti explained, 'You're correct. I don't personally know Swami, and I haven't studied Pramukh Swami's life in depth. However, there are many young disciples of his residing in this county. I noticed that there are no reports of domestic abuse among them, they are the first to arrive for community services when I call them, and they volunteer with dedication. Their exemplary character speaks volumes. Observing them, I realized that the greatness of their guru must be extraordinary.' Indeed, a life guided by strong values not only inspires, but also leaves a lasting legacy.

Yes, intelligence, talent, and experience are undoubtedly valuable assets. However, their influence can only take us so far. The development of values, stronger than steel, shields us from temptations and fortifies us against challenges. While our talents may propel us forward, it is our values that enable us to consistently perform at our best throughout the years and position us among the ranks of legends. As we explore what it truly means to lead with such values, we equip ourselves with the necessary tools to achieve success, security, stability, and fulfilment. In doing so, we may even leave a timeless legacy that resonates through generations.

THE WRIGGLING BUTTERFLY

Turbulent upbringings, crushing failures, suffocating fears: binding and darkening, they slowly drain our energy. Yet, for those who persist in their struggles, breaking free from their cocoon brings forth a transformation, making them stronger and more magnificent, elevating them to extraordinary heights. They say success does not come easy; the flight of the butterfly must be earned.

As the sun dipped low, painting the battlefield in golden hues, shadows danced across the weary warriors and the trampled earth, weighed down by the toll of four relentless days of battle. Amidst this solemn scene, Duryodhan, the formidable prince of the Kauravas, held his face in his hands and knelt in a state of bewildered contemplation. His kingdom boasted unparalleled wealth, his army outnumbered the opposition by 400,000 soldiers and 80,000 chariots, and his forces harboured some of the most skilled warriors in existence. Yet, despite these overwhelming advantages, he stood on the brink of defeat. A sense of personal indignation smouldered within him as he recollected the recent humiliation inflicted upon him by Arjun, whose skilled arrows had pierced Duryodhan's supposedly impenetrable armour mere hours before.

He wrestled with the relentless question echoing in his mind: 'Why me?' Despite wielding every conceivable advantage, why did he endure failure after failure on the battlefield? In this moment of vulnerability, Duryodhan sought solace from his trusted general, Dronacharya. 'Arjun and I were in the same class, studied the same subjects, and had the same teachers,' Duryodhan continued, 'So why has Arjun excelled repeatedly, while I have lagged behind?'

The general understood the true essence of the conflict. It wasn't merely a clash between two armies, but a struggle between two cousins. Cousins who had shared the same ancestry, kingdom, and training. Dronacharya, an uncle and teacher to both sides, had witnessed the kingdom's evolution and observed the growth of both sets of cousins.

In response, Dronacharya provided profound insights into their upbringing: Duryodhan, you have always been surrounded by the luxuries of the palace. Arjun, on the other hand, was born in the wilderness and endured exile from the kingdom on three occasions. While you savoured sumptuous cuisine crafted by the finest chefs, Arjun had to scavenge for firewood to ignite the stoves. While everyone attended to your every need, Arjun grappled with challenges independently. He thrived amidst adversity, whereas you, Duryodhan, were coddled. Arjun sought refuge in God, while you remain bound by worldly comforts. These differences ensure that he will always find success in any circumstance, while your potential will forever be constrained.

Hardship and struggle, often perceived as painful, are, in truth, the very essence of life's elixir. Just as a caterpillar must endure the arduous process of wriggling and squirming within its cocoon prison before emerging with the strength to spread its wings as a butterfly, so too must we struggle first if we aspire to reach great heights. However, those caterpillars that are 'assisted' out of their cocoons for a quicker and easier escape never subsequently acquire the necessary strength to soar. Instead, they remain helplessly squirming, winged insects forever grounded.

Many embark on the relentless pursuit of success, aiming to spread their wings and soar into the skies. However, this intense desire often leads us to seek shortcuts, hoping they will provide a smoother path to our goals. Fear of failure frequently grips us even before it materializes, steering us away from the more arduous routes ahead. The possibility of failure becoming intertwined with our very identity, and the shame it carries, weigh heavily on our minds, casting shadows over our aspirations. In our society, the tolerance for failure has diminished, and the expectation for instant gratification has become the norm.

However, if we aspire to soar, we must learn to embrace the struggle with patience and enthusiasm. For it is through the trials and failures along the way that we gain resilience, clarity, and growth. It's crucial to reassess our perception of failure and begin to see it as a stepping stone towards improvement. While failure may shape us, it also empowers us to evolve and excel. To adopt this mindset, we require proper guidance and support.

The answer lies back on the battlefield with Arjun. From the outset of the conflict, he grappled with the weight of past failures that led him to this war and a deep-seated fear of potential defeat on the battlefield. Despite these insecurities, his response showcased emotional maturity. Instead of suppressing his apprehensions, he turned to Bhagwan Krishna, a wise friend and confidant, with whom he could openly share his doubts, confusion, and inner turmoil. Arjun's willingness to acknowledge his vulnerabilities and seek guidance for solutions demonstrated emotional transparency—a pivotal initial step. Accepting and embracing one's emotions lay the foundation for constructive coping mechanisms.

After addressing the problem, Arjun developed a reflective nature by delving internally, seeking areas for self-improvement instead of deflecting blame onto external circumstances. He gracefully accepted Bhagwan Krishna's feedback, showing a willingness to learn and evolve. In contrast, Duryodhan, even when confronted, habitually shifted blame onto others and external factors. This reluctance to acknowledge his own issues prevented him from recognizing his flaws and hindered his personal growth.

Finally, Arjun adeptly translates these setbacks and guidance into actionable behaviours. His resilient upbringing stems from his proactive approach, transforming introspection into measures capable of surmounting future challenges. This stands in stark contrast to 'Duryodhan's passive demeanour that indulges in self-pity or external blame. Instead of dwelling on thoughts such as 'I am worthless', 'It's not fair', or 'Why did this happen to me?' Arjun adopts a constructive mindset, asking questions like 'What can I do to improve?' or 'Who can I ask for help?' This proactive attitude allows him to effectively navigate adversity and emerge stronger from each trial.

In short, Arjun's approach to failure encompasses emotional acceptance, constructive expression of doubts, self-reflection devoid of blame-shifting, and proactive steps toward improvement. His active engagement amidst adversity highlights a resilience that turns setbacks into stepping stones for personal and spiritual growth. Arjun's journey serves as a timeless guide for individuals navigating their failures, underscoring the transformative potential of a constructive and proactive mindset.

Ultimately, as Dronacharya elucidated, Arjun's unflinching faith in God served as his greatest strength. Unlike Duryodhan, who perceived failures as personal attacks and reflections of worldly injustices, Arjun's faith empowered him to perceive setbacks as integral parts of a larger divine plan. With the right guidance, he adopted a spiritual perspective that prioritized not just the outcomes of actions, but also how actions were carried out in the present moment. This perspective proved particularly invaluable during the war, where amidst the uncertainties of combat, Arjun remained focused on fulfilling his duties, performing his best, and heeding wise counsel, rather than dwelling on past failures or succumbing to future anxieties.

I learned this outstanding spiritual attitude from the life of Pramukh Swami Maharaj. In the 1980s, Swamiji envisioned the creation of a traditional stone temple in London to serve the Hindu community. On 16 October 1985, the local BAPS community, with the permission of the Greater London Council, purchased land in Harrow. However, they soon faced local opposition due to traffic concerns. Swamiji encouraged everyone to address the issue patiently, through open dialogue, public awareness, and prayers.

Following this advice, the BAPS volunteers engaged with the local community to increase awareness. As Swamiji continued to provide encouragement, a petition was diligently collected with over 20,000 signatures from the local residents. Everyone felt confident that their years of planning would result in a favourable outcome.

Unexpectedly, in February 1987, the building permission was denied due to environmental concerns. The BAPS community described this setback as a 'low point', 'devastating', and a 'heartbreaking end to our dreams'. However, when Swamiji was informed of the decision, his reaction was a picture of calm and stability. He remarked, 'God is the all-doer and acts for the best. We gave it our all, but now we must accept the result given to us. We have decided to build a temple in London, and we will. So, start looking for another piece of land. God will provide us with something better.'*

---

* BAPSChannel. 30 December 2021. 'Documentary Part 2. The First of Its Kind'. *YouTube*, https://tinyurl.com/mud5rmf3. (accessed 11 November 2024).

Behind Pramukh Swami Maharaj's dreams and efforts lay a bedrock of faith. This faith not only fuelled his resilience and stability, but also empowered the BAPS community to persist patiently. Eight years later, their perseverance culminated in the completion of a grand traditional temple in Neasden, London. Hailed by *Reader's Digest* as the eighth wonder of the world, the temple stands not just as an architectural marvel, but as a testament to the patience, peace, and perseverance of the devoted volunteers.*

In our journey through life, it's crucial to harness untapped sources of wisdom. In the professional realm, this could entail seeking guidance from senior colleagues who can serve as mentors, while also confiding in friends and family for essential personal support. Additionally, spirituality acts as a guiding light and source of comfort as we navigate unforeseen trials. By shifting our focus towards extracting growth from failures, we not only develop the resilience to accept setbacks, but also acquire invaluable insights to strengthen ourselves against future challenges.

---

* 24 February 1999. 'Wonder of the World'. *BAPS*, https://tinyurl.com/yj2arn67 (accessed 11 November 2024).

TEST OF THE TITANS

While it's natural to aspire, success often brings the allure of power, status, and wealth— temptations that can be hard to resist. Without a solid foundation of values, these temptations pose a significant risk of tainting our hard-earned reputation. How can we effectively navigate these potential pitfalls that have led to the downfall of corporate giants?

One of the most brilliant minds in the realm of business and finance was Harshad Mehta. Within ten years, he quickly rose to prominence in the Indian securities industry and was praised as the 'Amitabh Bachchan' of the stock market. Sadly, his name soon became associated with controversy as he faced lawsuits over alleged fraudulent activities. Regrettably, like Mehta, many such success stories result in controversy. What prompts individuals of such intelligence, capability, and prominence like Harshad Mehta to engage in dishonest practices? Were the consequences of their actions not apparent to them? Did they not realize the fundamental ethical implications of their choices? And yet, why did they proceed despite this knowledge?

Well, when considering it, moral and ethical considerations are often subjects of debate—what one person may view as morally wrong, another may consider perfectly acceptable. However, values are universal. What we value determines our moral compass. For instance, do you value honesty? Then you might find it morally unacceptable to lie for personal gain. On the other hand, do you value success? What lengths would you go to achieve success? Would the pursuit of success outweigh the importance of honesty in your eyes? Reflecting on these questions helps us understand the decisions made by once-respected figures like Harshad Mehta. If they had prioritized honesty and integrity over success and wealth, could they have avoided the fate they ultimately faced? As leaders and professionals navigating these moral grey areas daily, we must consider what values we hold dear and how they guide our actions.

To unravel this, let's delve deeper into the example of Harshad Mehta. Before becoming a renowned figure in the world of stock markets, Mehta was an ordinary individual. Legend has it that he arrived in Mumbai, embarking on his stock market journey with a mere 40 rupees in his pocket. Transitioning from obscurity to becoming the trusted authority on all matters concerning equities, Mehta captured the admiration of the Indian public. It was evident that he possessed ambition, demonstrating a willingness to start from scratch and ascend the ranks through hard work. This trait is common among many, isn't it? But when does ambition veer into dangerous territory? Clayton Christensen, a Harvard Business School professor renowned for teaching 'Good Management Theory and How It Is Built,' sheds light on this inquiry in his book, 'How Will You Measure Your Life?' On the final day of his class, Christensen poses three questions to his students, one of which is, 'How can I be sure I'll stay out of jail?'

'Though the last question sounds light-hearted,' he clarifies. 'It's not. Two of the 32 individuals in my Rhodes scholar class ended up behind bars. Jeff Skilling, of Enron notoriety, was a fellow classmate at HBS. These were good individuals, but something in their lives led them astray.'[*]

What is this 'something'?

Well, ambition itself is not inherently bad. It often begins with noble intentions—to excel in life, make a positive impact, support our families, and advance our careers. However, as we progress and assume greater responsibilities, the pressure can become overwhelming. These moments of growth and vulnerability serve as true tests of our ethics. If we lack self-awareness during this critical phase—failing to understand who we are and our underlying purpose—our once-nurtured ambition may morph into a relentless pursuit of success at any cost. This shift can lead us to compromise our integrity and embrace detrimental behaviours such as

---

[*] 'How Will You Measure Your Life?'. *Harvard Business Review*, https://tinyurl.com/7jkxzj78 (accessed 12 November 2024).

greed and temptation—the urge to achieve more, earn more, and become more, regardless of the consequences.

How can we rise above these moments of vulnerability? What actions can we take to curb these temptations before they take root?

As a professional and leader, understanding oneself becomes all the more important. Before we begin leading others, we must learn to lead ourselves. But how? Well, self-leadership entails mastering one's morals, emotions, and thoughts. Only after gaining a profound understanding of ourselves, our values, and our guiding principles can we effectively lead others. So, ask yourself: What do you truly value in life? List everything that comes to mind—family, career, education, friendships, health, wealth, possessions, time, spirituality, faith, kindness, fame, followers, honesty, fairness, and more. Now, can you prioritize them? It's challenging, but if forced to choose, which would you prioritize? Though seemingly unfair, knowing your priorities provides essential clarity on your core values. Without a robust grounding in values such as honesty and integrity, the allure of material possessions, fame, and power can easily lead you astray.

So how can we ensure that we lead an ethical life? Is it feasible to attain success without compromising our ethics?

Consider the case of Ratan Tata, the esteemed Indian industrialist, philanthropist, and former chairman of Tata Group. Once, the Tata Group entered into an MoU with an international company to establish a joint venture. Despite the completion of a new factory, they encountered a hurdle: no clients were placing orders. In a meeting, the CEO of the partner company, unaware of Tata Group's ethical corporate culture, proposed a dubious solution to Ratan Tata, 'We set up the factory, but we can't sell a single item. So, I hope it's all right if I, you know, deal with it.'

'No, it's not all right. How can you even ask such a question?' Ratan Tata responded incredulously.

'Then the factory will close down,' warned the CEO.

Tata remained steadfast, asserting, 'For that, if you must close it down, close it down. But we hired you because we thought you would get an honest order.'

The CEO was taken aback. Witnessing Ratan Tata's unwavering principles, he became optimistic about the possibility of achieving success without sacrificing integrity. With renewed motivation, he persevered and redoubled his efforts. Consequently, the company flourished without resorting to unethical practices.[*]

Now, coming back to Clayton Christensen's striking question: 'How can I be sure I'll stay out of jail?' What would you say? A litmus test is to ask yourself these questions: 'Have I ever justified wrongdoing simply because it was commonplace? Have I engaged in unethical behaviour because I thought no one would notice?' And if the answer is 'yes', then introspection is necessary. 'But it was a very small thing . . .' you may say, 'No one would even mind.' Yet, in matters of values and ethics, even the

---

[*] Shah, Shashank. 'Managing Difficult Situations', In *The Tata Group: From Torchbearers to Trailblazers*, pp. 270.

slightest deviation remains a deviation. Pramukh Swami Maharaj always emphasized: 'Don't do anything at the risk of breaking your ethics, norms, or disciplines.' Law enforcement penalizes any encroachment beyond the traffic crossing line. Regardless of magnitude, wrongdoing remains wrong, devoid of justification. We too must have clear boundaries.

Self-awareness marks the first step in constructing a robust ethical framework. As one continues to reflect, gain clarity, and strengthen values, we can embrace positive transformation. Then, by consistently adhering to principles, we cultivate resilience against temptations, earning the genuine trust and respect of colleagues. This will surely pave the way for your assured success.

So, what do you say? Is it possible to achieve success without compromising your ethics?

I say, absolutely yes.

THE PATH TO GREATNESS

Amidst the journey of life, it is a common occurrence for people to witness a fading enthusiasm for their jobs, slowly extinguishing the once vibrant spark within them. In these moments, many passively accept their challenging circumstances, succumbing to a sense of resignation or even nurturing feelings of resentment. However, amidst this backdrop, there exist exceptional individuals who rise above these challenges, fearlessly defying all odds. They boldly forge their paths to success, serving as living proof that greatness can be achieved regardless of the obstacles one encounters.

Greatness is not exclusive to a privileged few; it can be nurtured by the diligent. Pointing out the difference between the successful and ordinary, the renowned author and motivational speaker, Shiv Khera states, 'Winners don't do different things; they do things differently.'

Yes, the test of true success is not necessarily the amount of work one does, but how one does it. By observing the world around us, we come across numerous examples of people who have risen from obscurity to greatness through their unprecedented commitment, enthusiasm, and determination.

In the late 1800s, a time of innovation and discovery, the fountain pen emerged as a revolutionary tool. Amid this era of change, an unassuming figure named George Parker held an ordinary position at a fountain pen manufacturing company. However, these pens suffered from numerous defects, leaving disgruntled customers and an overwhelmed company unable to address the issues. Undeterred by the circumstances, driven by a deep desire to satisfy upset customers, George took it upon himself to repair the faulty pens at home.

Through his persistence and dedication, George soon acquired a very detailed understanding of fountain pens, surpassing even the expertise of the company itself. This newfound knowledge ignited a brilliant idea within him: what if I were to manufacture the pens myself? Fuelled by this revelation, he spent long hours and untiring efforts into turning his vision into reality. After numerous trials and stages of development, he succeeded in introducing the world to the iconic Parker pen.

Today, the company founded by this unassuming worker still stands tall as one of the leading manufacturers of fountain pens. It stands as a testament to the remarkable achievements that can arise from infusing ordinary tasks with extraordinary dedication.

Once, as Michelangelo was deeply engrossed in sculpting a magnificent statue, one of his friends arrived at his workshop. Filled with curiosity, the friend could not help but inquire, 'Michel, when I last visited you eight days ago, you were already working on this sculpture. Have you made any significant progress?'

Michelangelo calmly responded with a serene and focused demeanour, 'Indeed, my friend. In these eight days, I have meticulously refined the intricate details of the statue. I have delicately shaped the wrinkles upon the forehead, perfected the expression in the eyes, and even added a new line to trace an artery upon the face.'

Perplexed, the friend remarked, 'But Michel, these seem like simple adjustments.'

A gentle smile graced Michelangelo's lips as he replied, 'Ah, my dear friend, it is precisely these seemingly ordinary adjustments that bring any work to completion. Every subtle detail contributes to its ideal form.'

At that moment, the friend gained a newfound appreciation for the immense dedication and attention to detail that Michelangelo poured into his craft. For it is often the smallest of adjustments, the seemingly insignificant brushstrokes, or the delicate chisel marks that elevate a creation from mere potential to a masterpiece worthy of awe and admiration.

Whether creating a huge Akshardham complex or answering a trivial letter from a farmer—no matter how seemingly magnificent or mundane the task—Pramukh Swami Maharaj would embrace each duty with a profound sense of reverence and commitment.

Narendra Modi, reflecting on Swamiji's work ethic, eloquently explained, 'Even if the menial job of placing a brick on a mandir wall falls upon the shoulders of Pramukh Swami, he will do it with such care and devotion that it is akin to adorning the head of God with a majestic crown.'

Throughout history, individuals from diverse backgrounds have exemplified the power of unwavering commitment, transcending humble beginnings to great heights.

Consider Wellington, a humble cleaner in the British Parliament who rose to become the Mayor of London. Or Gillette, who once roamed the streets as a salesman and later became the owner of the renowned Gillette company. Similarly, Karsan Patel, who pedalled on his bicycle selling washing powder, went on to establish the successful Nirma company. And let's not forget Amitabh Bachchan, initially considered unfit for a radio jockey role, who eventually became a celebrated actor.

Just as each day presents us with unique opportunities, let us remember the words of Martin Luther King Jr, who notably uttered:

> If it falls your lot to be a street sweeper, sweep streets like Michelangelo painted pictures, sweep streets like Beethoven composed music, sweep streets like Leontyne Price sings before the Metropolitan Opera. Sweep streets like Shakespeare wrote poetry. Sweep streets so well that all the hosts of heaven and earth will have to pause and

say: Here lived a great street sweeper who swept his
job well.[*]

Numerous stories stand as a testament to the fact that
unwavering dedication is the defining factor in achieving
greatness. Let us become the authors of our own success
stories by wholeheartedly embracing our roles, and striving
for excellence in every endeavour, regardless of its magnitude
or simplicity. Through unwavering commitment and
relentless pursuit of brilliance, we carve our unique paths
to greatness.

---

[*] 2017. 'Martin Luther King Jr: An extraordinary life'. *The Seattle Times*,
https://tinyurl.com/mrpcyt4 (accessed 11 November 2024).

WORK-LIFE HARMONY

In today's whirlwind of demands and expectations, the modern professional faces a daunting challenge unlike any before. We're caught in a relentless cycle of 'busyness', stretching ourselves thin to keep pace with demands, and thus, risk losing sight of what truly matters. It's time to reclaim control, to forge a new path towards harmony and fulfilment, where success isn't measured by the number of plates we keep spinning, but by how seamlessly we embrace each moment.

In today's fast-paced world, the life of a working professional has undergone significant transformations compared to our grandparents' era. We find ourselves grappling with the constraints of limited time and energy, amidst an endless stream of tasks. It's like a waiter balancing an overwhelming number of plates, pushing ourselves to the brink, straining both body and mind, all while convincing ourselves that this frantic pace is only temporary. However, sooner or later, the strain becomes too much to bear, and something important inevitably slips through our grasp, shattering the delicate balance we've struggled to maintain. The repercussions of this imbalance can be profound and far-reaching. Relationships crumble, children are inadvertently neglected, and the very essence of our purpose becomes obscured.

Regrets, my friend, are not unheard of. Ask a dying person what they wish they would have done differently, and you may hear them saying, 'I wish I'd had the courage to live a life true to myself, not the life others expected of me', or, 'I wish I'd had the courage to express my feelings', or, 'I wish I had stayed in touch with my friends', or, 'I wish I had let myself be happier.' And, even, *I wish I hadn't worked so hard.'* It's important to understand that these aren't random phrases picked out of thin air. These refer to the 'top five regrets of the dying' as documented by former palliative care worker Bronnie Ware.*

Read the last regret again. It really hits hard. That's right. Consider this: we devote ten-twelve hours of our daily waking life, five to six days a week, to what? Work. Yet, as we face our mortality, what do we regret? Pouring so much of ourselves into it. We lament the time stolen from family time or pursuing our ultimate goals. Had we not toiled so relentlessly, perhaps we could have nurtured the people and lifestyle we care about most instead of drowning in guilt

---

* Ware, Bronnie. 'The Top Five Regrets of the Dying: A Life Transformed by the Dearly Departing'. *PMC*, https://tinyurl.com/3en6e9w7 (accessed 12 November 2024).

and regret. It begs the question: what kind of lifestyle robs us of our peace? What kind of existence leaves us devoid of contentment in the end?

While it's not always a matter of prioritizing one aspect over another or simplistically choosing between work and life (can we truly separate the two?), the solution is often more straightforward than we might expect. It revolves around how we structure our lives. Remember, life and work are not distinct entities; rather, work is just one element of our existence among many. So, how can we cultivate a lifestyle where we're not constantly torn between different elements and burdened by guilt? How can we create a harmonious coexistence of family, friends, work, hobbies, health, and faith so that we feel fulfilled and at ease with our decisions?

During the 172nd commencement speech at the Georgia Tech Institute on 6 September 1996, Brian Dyson, former CEO of Coca-Cola, delivered a brief yet profoundly inspiring address on life. He stated:

> Imagine life as a game in which you are juggling some five balls in the air. You name them work, family, health, friends and spirit. And you're keeping all of these in the air. You will soon understand that work is a rubber ball. If you drop it, it will bounce back. But the other four balls—family, health, friends and spirit—are made of glass. If you drop one of these, they will be irrevocably scuffed, marked, nicked, damaged or even shattered. They will never be the

same. You must understand that and strive for balance in your life.*

Certainly, there are moments when navigating these decisions feels overwhelmingly challenging. Prioritizing can become perplexingly complex. One day, you might tussle with financial stress, while on another, emotional turmoil may dominate. Yet, at the core lies the importance of recognizing your values and their significance. This awareness aids in discerning the choices that align with your true priorities, minimizing future regrets. Moreover, it's imperative to acknowledge that your hierarchy of values may diverge from others, and that's perfectly acceptable. In a society often fixated on external perceptions and conforming to societal norms— 'what will they think?'— remember that the consequences of your choices primarily impact you. As Dyson aptly emphasized in his speech, 'Don't set your goals by what other people deem important. Only you know what is best for you.'†

Successful individuals across various industries have come to realize the importance of achieving a harmonious balance between work and personal life, and have taken proactive steps to prioritize what truly matters to them. A striking example is the celebrated Bollywood superstar, Amitabh Bachchan. When his mother, Teji Bachchan, fell

---

* '5 balls of life commencement speech by Coca-Cola's ex-CEO Brian Dyson'. *Shine*, https://tinyurl.com/4rtpby68 (accessed 12 November 2024)
† '5 balls of life: speech by Coca Cola's former CEO'. *LinkedIn*, https://tinyurl.com/kvrmfwcz (accessed 12 November 2024).

ill and required hospitalization, Amitabh Bachchan spent an enormous amount of time caring for her. Simultaneously, Amitabh Bachchan maintained impeccable punctuality when filming, despite navigating through Mumbai's notorious traffic. Both as an actor and son, he managed to balance seamlessly, even when faced with logistical challenges.

Mahant Swami Maharaj is a shining example of a harmonious life. As the spiritual head of BAPS, he is dedicated to serving society and leading more than a million devotees in the spirit of selfless service spanning health awareness, education, humanitarian relief, environmental protection, and community empowerment. At the same time, he makes time in his daily routine to counsel people and answer hundreds of letters while also doing what gives one peace like devotion, meditation, reading sacred texts, and prayer. Amongst all of this, he ensures not to neglect his health, by regularly exercising and performing yoga with breathing exercises. When asked if he ever feels stressed by the enormity of his responsibilities, he answers that he feels burden-free by becoming a medium for God to perform tasks. He sees no distinction between service, devotion, and his daily routine. For him, it is all a harmonious spiritual experience with God.

While organizations often emphasize the concept of work-life balance, the term 'balance' implies a trade-off or sacrifice. In contrast, harmony suggests that work and all other aspects of personal life align and coexist synergistically, serving a greater purpose. Achieving work-life harmony within the complex structure of a corporate environment may seem daunting, but employing what I call the '3P Method' can pave the way for a more balanced existence.

Firstly, it's essential to clarify and continually refine your **purpose**. What are your core values and passions? By anchoring your life, including your career, to a greater purpose, every task becomes a source of fulfilment rather than a drain on your energy. Consider what drives you each day—whether it's securing your children's future, contributing something positive to society, or serving a higher calling. Understanding your 'big why' provides a compass for navigating life's challenges.

Secondly, effective **people** management is crucial. Resist the urge to prioritize people-pleasing at the expense of your well-being or other priorities. Establish clear personal and professional boundaries, recognizing that while social obligations and work expectations are important, they should never overshadow the needs of your closest relationships. Learning to say no and letting go of unnecessary burdens is key. Surround yourself with a supportive network of family, friends, and mentors who understand your ambitions and offer genuine support when needed.

Lastly, **prioritize** with precision. Set clear goals that align with both your personal values and professional aspirations. Distinguish between what's truly important and what merely seems urgent, avoiding the trap of neglecting the significant in favour of the immediate. Dedicate regular time to your health, family, and spiritual growth, recognizing their enduring importance. Practice context switching rather than multitasking, allowing yourself to transition seamlessly between different responsibilities without sacrificing focus or succumbing to stress. By embracing these principles, you can begin a new chapter characterized by harmony, purpose, and fulfilment.

Today, author Bronnie Ware proudly declares a life free of regrets.[*] It took Ware's entire career in palliative care and sincere reflection to find freedom from the guilt of regrets. And so, if you are reading this, there is still time. Time to learn from others who have failed or seen others fail and those who have succeeded. At the end of the day, do you want to end your life full of regrets? Or, are you ready to take the necessary steps to live a fulfilling life?

---

[*] *Bronnie Ware*, https://tinyurl.com/2p8yjmak (accessed 12 November 2024).

YOU'RE ON MUTE

Have you ever been left on mute, passionately discussing something, only to discover that no one is listening? It's infuriating. What should you do? Shout? Wave your arms? Call people out? None of these seem ideal. In this noisy, information-saturated world, shouting louder won't attract an audience. Loud demonstrations don't always guarantee attention either. Instead, we need to move beyond mere words to make a real impact.

'You're on mute.' These words became a cultural icon during the COVID-19 pandemic as the world went online. The phrase appeared on t-shirts, coffee mugs, and mousepads. It became a popular meme on the internet, poking fun at those awkward moments when someone was speaking into the void because they forgot to unmute. Even Zoom's CEO, Eric Yuan, once forgot to unmute himself on a call with investors. Interestingly, this isn't just a virtual phenomenon. It happens in real life, too—when we share something meaningful only to realize no one is paying attention, as if we're on mute.

Why does it happen that people don't listen, even when you're speaking about something important? And how can you change that to get people to pay attention? The simple answer is that everyone wants to be heard. Whether you're a parent, teacher, employee, spouse, coach, or politician, feeling ignored is a deeply unsettling experience. There's almost nothing more dehumanizing than having your thoughts and feelings dismissed. So, to ensure others listen to you, start by stepping into their shoes. Ask yourself: What are they feeling? What are their concerns? When you take the time to listen to others, they are more likely to listen to you in return. In other words, if you want people to hear you, you first need to learn to hear them.

Why is it so hard for us to pause and listen? Listening requires practice, patience, courage, and humility. It's challenging because humans are inherently self-centric, often consumed by our own lives, problems, ambitions, and perceptions of self-image. This focus on ourselves leaves little room to create genuine connections through meaningful conversations rather than just skimming the surface with superficial exchanges.

Additionally, we aren't typically trained to listen. While reading and writing are emphasized from childhood, listening skills aren't given the same importance in formal education. There's a notable gap in teaching what it means to be a good listener, let alone how to listen effectively. As a result, many of us don't develop the skills needed to truly engage with others, leading to a lack of meaningful dialogue and connection.

How can we listen better? Truly effective listening involves respect, empathy, and careful attention, with a focus on authentic, meaningful communication. Once, in Mumbai, Pramukh Swami Maharaj was approached by a father. He wanted Swamiji to name his son. Naming a child is a significant moment, and the father trusted Swamiji to choose a name with the right sound and meaning. As part of the process, Swamiji asked the father for his son's 'rashi', which is traditionally used to determine the starting sound of a name. The father wasn't sure, so Swamiji asked more questions, deduced the rashi, and suggested that the name could start with 'M' or 'T'.

After some thought, Swamiji recommended the name 'Mayank'. The father hesitated briefly, but Swamiji noticed the pause and immediately asked, 'How about "Mayur" instead?' The father enthusiastically agreed, 'That's perfect!' In that split second, Swamiji immediately grasped the significance of the father's silence. This ability to understand what wasn't explicitly said is why thousands of people listened to Swamiji, because he truly listened to them—with love, intent, and empathy. To become a better listener, it's crucial to pay attention to the subtle cues: the pauses, the tone of voice, and the expressions on people's faces. These cues reveal more than words alone. To listen well, we must focus carefully on all these elements and learn to hear the unspoken.

Another way to make yourself heard is to offer something of genuine value. People are more likely to pay attention when you have something meaningful to contribute. A popular piece of advice is, 'Don't raise the volume of your voice, but raise the value of your words.' This means that if you're not enhancing the quality of the discussion, it's better to remain silent. Before speaking, it's essential to understand the mindset of everyone involved in the conversation. Listen to the flow and the topic of discussion. Be patient, wait for the right moment, and then share something valuable. It's not always about providing a solution or stating your opinion. Sometimes, asking a thoughtful question can change the entire dynamic of a conversation.

Pramukh Swami Maharaj wisely advised that when starting a new role, working in a new place, or engaging in a new community, it's wise to spend the first year or two simply listening, observing, and building connections. During this time, you can earn people's respect and friendship, while also gaining a deeper understanding of the challenges. Only after establishing this rapport and securing the backing of senior colleagues should you begin to offer suggestions or share your ideas.

Unfortunately, corporations often place more emphasis on speaking up and being visible than on the actual substance behind the words. But as leaders, it's crucial to recognize and value those who genuinely contribute to the company's success. These individuals might speak less but are often doing just as much, if not more, than those who make a show of their work. The great American philosopher, Ralph Waldo Emerson, once remarked, 'What you are shouts so loudly in my ears that I cannot hear what you're saying.' Similarly, Benjamin Franklin, one of the Founding Fathers of the United States, stated, 'Well done is better than well said.' These insights suggest that while some people might be loud and put on a grand performance, the true impact comes from actions, not just words. The best leaders understand that those who quietly make a difference are as valuable as— or even more so than—those who seek the spotlight.

In 1974, during the inauguration of the first BAPS mandir in North America, Pramukh Swami Maharaj was in the New York City with another respected Hindu leader. During the ceremony, this leader remarked, 'I have been coming to America for years and still haven't been able to build a permanent place of worship. Yet, Pramukh Swami has just inaugurated a mandir on his first visit—how is it possible?'

Later, when Pramukh Swami Maharaj stepped onto the stage, he noticed that the sacred image of Bhagwan Swaminarayan had been placed on a small, plain seat, while his own seat was more ornate. Without hesitation or words, Pramukh Swami Maharaj immediately switched seats, taking the smaller, simpler seat for himself. The other Hindu leader witnessed this action and commented, 'Just this morning, I asked how he could build a temple in America. Now, I have my answer.' Pramukh Swami Maharaj didn't need to speak about devotion or humility—his actions demonstrated it perfectly.

It's said of Cicero, who served under Julius Caesar, that when Cicero spoke, people applauded; but when Caesar spoke, they followed him into battle. Similarly, Pramukh Swami Maharaj was a man of few words, yet his messages resonated deeply. When he spoke, people resolved conflicts, reconciled with family, renounced materialistic lifestyles, and abandoned harmful habits and addictions. This is because people are more likely to follow what you do than what you say.

A religious reformer in Anand, Gujarat, once explained, 'Why do people not heed our words, but why do Pramukh Swami Maharaj's words make an impact?' He likened it to writing a cheque. When a bank account has no funds, a cheque bounces. If our words lack character, they carry no weight. In contrast, Pramukh Swami Maharaj's words had a high 'bank balance' of character, giving them considerable influence and impact. This analogy reveals a profound truth: the power of speech means little if the words themselves lack virtue and authenticity. When words are backed by integrity, they can transform lives and inspire action.

So, the next time you, as a parent, wonder why your children aren't listening to you, or why your employee is being stubborn, or if you ever feel like you're on mute, pause and ask yourself, 'Am I listening enough? Am I listening genuinely and empathetically? Do I understand my audience? Are my words backed by my actions?' And, therein, you may find your answer.

PUTTING PEOPLE FIRST

In roles of power and authority, it's easy to become consumed with delivering results, inadvertently overlooking what truly motivates people. However, employees are no longer silent bystanders. They're increasingly vocal about injustices, toxic cultures, and unfair policies. So, how might organizations react? Is it possible for leaders to prioritize their people in a way that fosters a supportive environment and ensures sustained success?

Workplaces underwent a striking transformation in 2020, propelled by the global spread of a deadly virus, infamously known as Covid-19. This virus, while confining millions worldwide to the shelter of their homes, also acted as a catalyst for change. It exposed flaws in corporate culture, highlighted stark policies, and prompted a re-evaluation of longstanding corporate practices. As the world emerged from the pandemic, these discussions and voices only grew louder. From calls for flexible working hours to protests against dehumanizing lay-off practices, the very fabric of organizational structures, particularly within large-scale corporations, has been called into question. At the heart of it all lies fundamental questions: What do employees truly desire? What are the underlying needs that their demands seek to address? And how can corporations effectively respond?

Well, we can start by acknowledging that people are the building blocks of society. Adam Smith, the founder of modern economics, recognized land, labour, and capital as the key factors of production required to create goods and services that make up any economy.* Without these, it would be impossible to run an economy. Likewise, people are the building blocks of any organization. Without them, there is no organization. It suffices to say, then, that people are a company's greatest asset. Yet, why are they so often not treated like one? Perhaps, what our society and workplaces need today are leaders and people in positions of authority who can recognize those below them for who they are—human beings with needs and desires yearning to be heard—and help them flourish. Simply put, what corporations need today are leaders who can prioritize their people.

'What about profits?' you ask. Well, profits shall follow.

Take, for instance, Pramukh Swami Maharaj. Through his emphasis on prioritizing people, he sparked a worldwide

---

* Fernando, Jason, '4 Factors of Production Explained with Examples'. *Investopedia*, https://tinyurl.com/6xyad36j (accessed 12 November 2024).

movement toward virtuous, dedicated, and selfless volunteerism. He often said, 'In the good of others, lies our own. In the joy of others, lies our own. In the progress of others, lies our own.' Not only did he preach this, but he also practiced it. The depth to which he reached out to people left a lasting impact.

During his tenure as Chief Minister of Gujarat, Shri Narendra Modi came to seek Pramukh Swami Maharaj's blessings at the BAPS Mandir in Ahmedabad. As the chief minister, protocol dictated he travel with an extensive convoy, which included armoured cars, police vehicles, and other supporting units. After meeting Pramukh Swami Maharaj, the Chief Minister returned to the car with a box of prasad in his hand.* However, as he was about to sit in the car, a small packet on the car dashboard caught his eye. He turned to face the swami accompanying him and asked, 'Has the prasad reached here as well?'

The swami replied, 'Sir, Pramukh Swami Maharaj always worries and says that those people who can come to meet us, of course they are attended to. But there will also be so many people with you who cannot leave their duty and they cannot come inside. What about them? So long before you received your prasad, every car, every driver, and every security officer has already received their packet of prasad.' Intrigued, the chief minister got down from his

---

* Prasad is a devotional offering of food to God, that is later distributed or shared amongst devotees after being sanctified; https://tinyurl.com/2f96fybu (accessed 12 November 2024).

car and went to check the other car and the third car, and all of them had a prasad box on their dashboard. That's when he turned around and exclaimed, 'Pramukh Swami never forgets the smallest of the small.' Truly, he was the people's leader.

However, if we embrace a people-centric approach, can we truly balance everyone's satisfaction while also prioritizing the organization's best interests? Let's be clear: people-centric leadership is not an oxymoron. Former US President Bill Clinton once noted that while many have risen by pushing others down, Pramukh Swami Maharaj elevated himself by lifting people up. So, there are indeed real-life examples of leaders who don't rely on exerting power. It's possible for a leader to successfully adopt a people-first approach. Those who prioritize people can undoubtedly become successful leaders. **Both can coexist.** How can we put this principle into action? What does it entail?

People-centricity doesn't require grand gestures or emotional strain. It can manifest in the simplest of acts, such as actively seeking the opinions of junior employees during a team meeting and taking relevant action. But why bother considering the suggestion of a young child, you might ask? After all, 'What do they know, right?' Wrong. A young child once slipped a piece of paper into Pramukh Swami Maharaj's hands, with a simple message: 'Swamiji, your seat was too high. I couldn't properly meet or take blessings from you. Please, next time, could you keep your seat a little lower?' Swamiji not only noted the contents of the note, but also later discussed the note with trustees and ensured his seat was accessible to even the smallest child.

Similar instances occur in the corporate world, where young children write to CEOs and receive constructive replies. Take the example of ambitious 10-year-old Alex Jacquot, who wrote a letter to the CEO of Qantas, the largest airline in Australia, about his dream to start his own airline.* Instead of dismissing the letter as just a childish dream and a waste of his time, Alan Joyce, the CEO, took time out to not just draft a reply but also invite Alex to exchange notes on how to run an airline. Or consider seven-year-old Chloe Bridgewater, who wrote a job application to Sundar Pichai, the CEO of Google, who responded with an inspiring message saying, 'I'm glad that you like computers and robots, and hope that you will continue to learn about technology [. . .] I think if you keep working hard and following your dreams, you can accomplish everything you set your mind to.'†

It doesn't stop there, though. When nine-year-old Eleanor Waterman discovered that the trousers she had bought from Tesco had fake pockets, she wrote an annoyed letter to CEO Dave Lewis demanding why boys' trousers had real pockets and hers didn't. How did they react? Along with a Tesco gift card, a representative wrote back,

---

* 'Qantas CEO: 10-yr-old boy writes to Qantas CEO about setting up airline, gets a reply—and Twitter goes wild!'. *The Economic Times*, https://tinyurl.com/3jxj9r5p (accessed 12 November 2024).

† 'Sundar Pichai responds to 7-year-old who asked for job'. *CNN*, https://tinyurl.com/m8tc4p7w (accessed 12 November 2024).

apologizing and promising to offer a more inclusive option to both boys and girls in the future.* It's worth considering, would we be willing to go to such lengths to address the concerns of our younger members?

Moreover, prioritizing people means transitioning from merely fulfilling your job duties or managing tasks to genuinely caring for those around you and safeguarding their interests. Do you invest enough time in conversing with your team members and understanding their needs? Do they feel listened to and valued? Are you familiar with their aspirations, motivations, and concerns? And if so, do you take action? Do you address their fears and aspirations and foster an environment conducive to their growth?

As someone in a position of power and authority, you have both the right and the responsibility to ensure that your organization's policies evolve to meet the needs of your people. Maternity leave was not always a standard practice; it became accepted because a leader somewhere empathized with mothers and recognized the necessity for change. By prioritizing your employees' well-being, you inspire them to dedicate their time and energy to the organization.

Expressing empathy is another effective way of placing others ahead of you and at the centre. Consider the instance when Pramukh Swami Maharaj, as the host, was willing to move an entire event venue for one person's comfort. Upon learning that the guest of honour, Swami Chidanandaji from

---

* 'Child writes to Tesco CEO to demand pockets for girls' school trousers'. *Metro*, https://tinyurl.com/34n67nem (accessed 12 November 2024).

Divine Life Society, had a fever, Pramukh Swami Maharaj insisted that the outdoor event be moved indoors, solely to ensure Swami Chidanandaji would not feel cold. When Swami Chidanandaji arrived, Pramukh Swami Maharaj draped him with a shawl he had kept specially for him. This act underscores the depth of his concern and his ability to empathize with others' needs. Whether addressing the needs of the most junior members or those in prominent positions, prioritizing others is essential for fostering organizations of the future.

During a convocation ceremony, Ratan Tata imparted his wisdom to management graduates: 'As you venture into the commercial world, my 40 years of experience in the corporate realm have taught me one crucial lesson that I'd like to share with you.' He explained, 'Do not measure your success by the luxuries you accumulate in your home or the balance in your bank account. Instead, gauge your success by the number of lives you have enriched during your journey as a human being on this earth.'

In today's leadership landscape, we must acknowledge and embrace the evolving needs of both present and future workplaces and their inhabitants. By prioritizing our people, actively engaging as listeners, investing in their development and empowerment, and demonstrating genuine empathy, we can effectively address these needs. When individuals feel heard, valued, and appreciated, they are more inclined to reciprocate positively. If every leader commits to nurturing these qualities, we can envision a future where workplaces become more welcoming, compassionate, and fulfilling for all.

SWEAT OF THE BROW

You don't just value a tree by its visible fruits; you also appreciate the strength of the unseen roots that anchor it. Similarly, within our careers, we are always looking for the next step up: we seek opportunity, we seek shortcuts, and we seek success. But maybe we need to dig a little deeper and work a little harder to gain something more profound.

The trajectory of society's advancement has been guided by ingenious thinking and this evolution has ushered humanity into an era of heightened efficiency and sophistication. We identified obstacles hindering our progress and cleverly devised strategies to overcome them. In modern workplaces, intelligent applications such as AI serve as invaluable allies, enabling workers to transcend the constraints of time and utilize their resources more effectively. Why invest precious time in memorizing routes when Google Maps can effortlessly guide us? Why expend energy on drafting emails when AI applications can perform the task with ease?

Smart solutions liberate us from mundane chores, allowing us to focus our energies on more significant tasks. By harnessing the power of smart thinking, we've effectively mitigated inefficiencies in our daily tasks, placing creativity and productivity at the forefront of our endeavours.

As we prioritize efficiency over the traditional value of hard work, it prompts us to ponder whether something essential is being lost in the process. The insightful words attributed to Sheikh Ahmed Zaki Yamani, a Saudi politician, encapsulate this sentiment: 'My grandfather rode a camel. My father drove a car. I fly in jet planes. My son will drive a car. My grandson will ride a camel.'* Yamani's narrative begins with a story of progress, illustrating how each successive generation toiled diligently and thus enjoyed greater convenience and comfort than the last. Yet, Yamani's advice to future generations is clear: despite the privileges gifted to them, they must not forget the ethos of hard work that enabled their predecessors to enjoy such luxury. By doing so, they can ensure that the opportunities they inherit are not squandered, but rather built upon.

Such an attitude has been adopted by a royal in North India. In the Indian state of Rajasthan, the Udaipur Palace serves as a heritage hotel, with its majestic white walls and gleaming architecture enchanting all who pass through its gates. Leading the royal family that has governed the

---

* *Oxford Essential Quotations*, Edited by Susan Ratcliffe. Oxford University Press. 2017.

palace for centuries is Prince Lakshyaraj Singh Ji Mewar. Despite his family's prestigious legacy within the palace, Prince Lakshyaraj chose to explore the hospitality trade from the ground up during his studies, working as a waiter and cleaning dishes as part of his training at a restaurant. He acknowledges these years as the 'most challenging' of his life, yet also the 'most memorable and rewarding', laying the foundation for his successful career.[*] While he could have easily commenced his career as a CEO or owner of his family's hotel, he found deeper meaning, clarity, and fulfilment in learning lessons along the way.

From legendary sports figures to top CEOs, talent undoubtedly grants individuals a platform to shine, but it is their relentless efforts that propel them to greatness. Consider the iconic cricketer Sachin Tendulkar. His journey from a budding talent to a cricketing legend is distinguished by the countless hours he devoted to perfecting his techniques and refining his skills. Beyond the glitz of receiving numerous accolades and the fame of international stardom, Tendulkar's story reveals a man who committed himself tirelessly from dawn to dusk to excel in his craft. Fondly reminiscing about his cricketing days, he recalls spending 'as much time on the field as possible' and 'training and playing for 12 hours a day'.[†] He frequently emphasizes that while luck may have played some role in his success, it was his relentless

---

[*] Lakshyarajsinghmewar, https://tinyurl.com/kcjs6ath (accessed 11 November 2024).

[†] 'Never Expose Your Weakness: Sachin Tendulkar'. *Times of India*, https://tinyurl.com/jrfbfchy (accessed 12 November 2024).

practice that primed him to seize opportunities when they arose. This ethos is one that Tendulkar passes on to his son, advising him, 'When you work hard, luck swings your way. There will be challenges in life, but with hard work, you can overcome them.'*

Hard work isn't just vital for technology and innovation; it's the backbone of all aspects of our lives. No shortcuts or efficiency can ever replace consistent dedication. Take, for instance, the pursuit of fitness. While investing in the latest sports technology, hiring top-notch personal trainers, and stocking up on supplements may seem like shortcuts to success, true progress only comes through the discipline of an active lifestyle and healthy habits. Smart accessories may enhance the journey, but their effectiveness is limited without a genuine commitment to putting in the necessary work.

During the scorching Indian summer months, Pramukh Swami Maharaj reached the village of Karchaliya, travelling from house to house, connecting with each of the town's residents and uplifting people from all walks of life. The relentless midday sun caused everyone's foreheads to glisten with sweat as they continued their travels. At one particular house, a sizable gathering had congregated. The homeowner eagerly approached Swamiji and began recounting an astonishing phenomenon: inside their home, a sacred image

---

* 'Hard work, commitment key to earn respect from others: Sachin Tendulkar'. *Times of India*, https://tinyurl.com/y6f2mx9m (accessed 12 November 2024).

consistently dripped nearly a full glass of water every day, drawing astonished onlookers from distant places. Hearing the homeowner's story, Swamiji responded with a desire to impart a lesson more profound than miracles. Wiping the sweat from his brow, Swamiji emphasized, 'Only this water'—the result of genuine hard work—'is truly useful.'

This remark may seem subtle, but its impact is profound. Throughout various aspects of life—academic, social, or spiritual—we often seek easy solutions, hoping for a quick fix to overcome challenges. We tend to overlook the value of hard work, opting instead for small 'miracles' that promise to make our lives easier. Swamiji dedicated seven decades, travelling to 250,000 homes, meeting over four million people across 60 countries. His life taught that there are no shortcuts in love and care.

A dedicated life also inspires the same in others, and I witness this profound impact each time I visit the simple village of Sarangpur, India, where a BAPS Hindu monastic centre thrives. Amidst the backdrop of majestic temples and echoing peacock calls, almost 300 swamis in training greet the early hours to start their daily routines. Guided by the vision of Mahant Swami Maharaj, these young aspirants undergo a rigorous seven-year programme of spiritual, academic, and personal development.

It's striking to note that many of these swamis hail from privileged backgrounds, having been raised in affluent families across America and England. Educated at esteemed institutions including Ivy League colleges, some even held positions at tech giants such as Amazon and Google. Yet, they willingly relinquished these luxuries in pursuit of a life dedicated to service, participating in over 160 different kinds of social, educational, medical, environmental, cultural, and religious activities for the benefit of society at large.

In contrast to their past lives of convenience, the swamis now embrace a simpler existence. They reject modern conveniences, opting instead for daily rituals such as washing clothes by hand, sweeping the temple grounds, and humble devotion. Formerly accustomed to wearing the latest fashion trends, they now possess only two sets of simple garments and opt for modest sandals instead. Their deliberate rejection of comforts underscores their commitment to a path that is both arduous and deeply fulfilling. This holistic preparation equips them to then traverse communities, offering their lives in service to God and society.

A young swami hailing from Canada shared with me:

I emerged from a life where everything seemed predestined—I had a car, house, and a promising career as a pilot. Yet, I willingly gave up these comforts because the teachings of my guru instilled in me the desire to contribute to a cause greater than myself. Through the grace of God, I've come to understand that embracing a disciplined lifestyle, one that includes cooking, cleaning, and spiritual practices, makes us self-sufficient and cultivates a growth mindset. This journey teaches us not only to value the labours of others, but also to remain resilient in the face of any adversity. Whether confronted with familiar tasks or thrust into uncharted territories, we stand prepared to confront challenges head-on. Devotion and service not only strengthen character, but also empower us to contribute more to the world.

All professionals aspire for success. It is the reason most wake up early in the morning and sleep late at night. While shortcuts and clever strategies may propel us to a certain level, it is the dedication invested behind the scenes that truly propels individuals toward achievement. As poet Henry Wadsworth Longfellow eloquently expresses, 'The heights by great men reached and kept were not attained by sudden flight, but they while their companions slept, were toiling upward in the night.'

Instead of merely seeking quick fixes, let's embrace opportunities that challenge, teach, and nurture personal growth. It's the wealth of experiences gained through diligence and dedication that best prepares us for the journey ahead. Far from fading, hard work will always stand as the trademark of successful and content individuals, serving as a steadfast companion on the path to a fulfilling and meaningful life.

THE DISHWASHING PRESIDENT

Who is a true leader? They don't push, pull, or drag; they simply lead, inspire, and effortlessly gain followers. The leaders we admire—the ones we discuss, immortalize in books, and even celebrate in song—are those who transcend titles to capture our hearts. True leadership, it appears, thrives not in dominating the boardroom, but in the humble yet determined souls who pave the way forward.

Over the decades, leadership has remained a subject of constant debate, fostering ongoing dialogue and differing opinions. As employees ascend the corporate ladder and assume managerial roles, they are entrusted with the task of 'leading' a team. However, lacking adequate training, constructive feedback mechanisms, and self-awareness, many organizations inadvertently promote individuals into formal leadership positions who harbour misconceptions about the essence of leadership. Suddenly thrust into positions of power and authority, these individuals are tasked with the responsibility of driving productivity and achieving collective objectives. What unfolds in such scenarios? Frequently, we encounter two distinct types of leaders situated at opposite ends of the spectrum. On one end, there are micromanagers—those who struggle to transition from being a worker to a manager, stifling their teams with excessive control. On the other end, we find proponents of laissez-faire management, who advocate for granting complete autonomy to their teams, often resulting in aimless wandering without guidance.

But where does the optimal balance lie? At what juncture does a manager transform into a true leader?

Let's take a step back and examine the current landscape of leadership. While job descriptions and human resources guidelines often emphasize the importance of empathy and awareness of employees' well-being, the reality as perceived by those on the ground can be starkly different. Surprisingly, happiness research reveals that the time people least enjoy during their week is often when they're interacting with their boss.[*] Startling, isn't it?

As a manager, you may find yourself thinking, 'Surely, my team wouldn't say that.' But can you be certain? It's crucial to take a moment to reflect. Do you notice a pattern of needing to repeat instructions? Do you feel compelled

---

[*] 'Happiness and Work: An interview with Lord Richard Layard'. *McKinsey*, https://tinyurl.com/efr3u53t (accessed 12 November 2024).

to frequently assert authority? Do you believe respect should be given simply because of your managerial title, or earned through actions? The prevalent 'boss mentality' that permeates many workplaces inadvertently fosters an atmosphere of anxiety and stress, causing employees to dread coming to work.

So, what's the solution?

Simple. What is the opposite of ordering, being loud, and demanding respect? How about sparking inspiration, remaining humble, and giving respect? Instead of pushing and pulling people to get work done, can we take them along with us? Simply, we need leaders who can lead with a humane approach. We need leaders who can be *servant leaders.*

Servant leaders? Yes.

The concept of 'servant leadership' was coined by Robert K. Greenleaf in 1970, although the essence of this leadership style has existed long before the term itself.[*] At its core, servant leadership embodies humility, prioritizing service to others over self-interest. It involves leading by example, emphasizing the strengths of others rather than focusing on weaknesses, listening attentively before giving orders, and prioritizing long-term benefits over short-term gains. These distinctive qualities characterize servant leadership, and they are all skills that can be cultivated through practice.

---

[*] 'What is Servant Leadership?'. *Greenleaf Center for Servant Leadership*, https://tinyurl.com/ycyxbz24 (accessed 12 November 2024).

Historical and contemporary figures alike have demonstrated that leading by serving produces enduring outcomes. Be it Nelson Mandela, Abdul Kalam, or Pramukh Swami Maharaj, these figures could unite and lead thousands towards a common cause and purpose, all the while asking, 'What can I give?' By cultivating a deep sense of responsibility and care towards others, they could accomplish in a shorter span what otherwise may have taken years to reach.

I witnessed effective leadership in the life of Pramukh Swami Maharaj as did countless others. On 21 May 1950, Swamiji was ordained president of the BAPS Sanstha at the young age of 28. It was a historic day for the fellowship. A gathering was organized in Ahmedabad to celebrate this occasion, with dinner arranged for all the guests. As per his nature, Pramukh Swami Maharaj chose to eat last. As he headed to the kitchen, what did he see? A pile of used dishes and utensils met his sight. In that moment, Swamiji, newly ordained as the organization's president, could have easily commanded someone to clean up the mess. Yet, he chose a different path—a path of humility and service. Without a word, he sat down and began washing the dishes himself. He didn't seek assistance; he simply took action. This act of selfless service on his very first day as a formal leader with authority left a profound impact. Since then, millions of people have been inspired by this quiet yet powerful gesture, and continue to emulate this attitude in their daily lives. It stands as a testament to the enduring strength of servant leadership, empowering 80,000 BAPS volunteers worldwide to serve with humility.

John C. Maxwell, a *New York Times* bestselling American author on leadership, once wrote, 'A leader is one who knows the way, goes the way, and shows the way.'[*] Indeed, many may offer advice and claim leadership, but true leadership requires the dedication and bravery to lead by example. It demands the willingness to embody one's words with action.

In 1967, BAPS organized a festival in Gondal, Gujarat. The residential school opposite the BAPS Mandir in Gondal was to be temporarily used for guests' lodging, and extensive repairs were under way for this purpose. As the convenor of the festival, Pramukh Swami Maharaj visited the site to assess the progress. To his surprise, much work remained, and time was running short before the event date. As the 'person in charge' here, he could have shouted orders at the workers to pick up speed. He could have reprimanded and re-engaged them. Hence, contrary to what traditional leadership emulates, he chose a different approach. He led by example. Not only did he *show the way*, but he also *went the way* by shouldering a pile of twelve tiles and carrying them up the stairs. Witnessing his actions, the workers were immediately inspired to increase their pace and become more engaged in their tasks. They looked upon their work with renewed enthusiasm and dedication. In the spirit of servant leadership, Pramukh Swami Maharaj led by giving first and giving from a place of love.

---

[*] *Goodreads*, https://tinyurl.com/yseu9x6n (accessed 12 November 2024).

As the poet Kabir beautifully expressed in one of his verses, 'While many strive for greatness, not all are willing to stoop low. Yet, it's often the ones who humble themselves the most who rise the highest.' How you conduct yourself, your interactions with others, and the attitude you adopt, all play significant roles when practicing servant leadership. Do you seek others' opinions, or do you impose your own views upon them? This distinction is crucial.

William McKnight, a top-class management guru who served as the president and chairman of the American company '3M' for decades, faced a significant challenge when he took the helm of the company during a period of near-bankruptcy. However, under his leadership, 3M flourished into a multi-billion-dollar revenue-generating entity. Drawing from his extensive experience collaborating closely with employees, McKnight shared invaluable insights: 'Present your ideas very softly to your people.' He emphasized the importance of creating an environment of empowerment and trust, stating, 'If you put fences around people, you get sheep. Give the people the room they need.' By granting individuals the autonomy they require and making them feel respected and valued, they are more likely to take ownership of their responsibilities and actively contribute to the organization's success.

In life, all of us will hold some kind of position of authority. Yet, the lessons from great leaders remind us of an alternative approach: prioritizing service through our actions, words, and deeds. By embodying qualities such as inspiration, humility, and respect, we naturally inspire others. True leadership isn't merely about holding a position; it's about making a meaningful impact and guiding others through genuine connection and example.

BE BIG-MINDED

In everyday life, be it with family or at work, we often find ourselves clinging onto grievances, both big and small. These perceived hurts can lead us to either distance ourselves from the source or harbour feelings of retribution. However, history's great figures have shown us the immense peace and benefits that come from being magnanimous. So, what does it mean to be big-minded, and how can we embody this in our lives?

Let me share with you the remarkable journey of Candice Mama, who lost her father to violence at just eight months old. Growing up, she cherished the fragments of memories she had, picturing her father as a vibrant soul, always smiling and dancing to his favourite tunes. Yet, there was a shadow over her understanding; whenever visitors glimpsed a particular book her mother kept, their reactions puzzled her. They would often break into tears or even screams.

One fateful day, while her mother was out, nine-year-old Candice's curiosity got the better of her. She climbed up onto a chair and retrieved the mysterious book from the top of her mother's cupboard. As she flipped through its pages, she stumbled upon a haunting image: a man, charred and clinging to a steering wheel, unmistakably her father. But the revelation didn't stop there. The book, titled *Into the Heart of Darkness: Confessions of Apartheid's Assassins*, laid bare the chilling details of her father's murder, attributing it to a figure known as 'Prime Evil'.

Realizing the gravity of the situation, Candice made a pivotal decision to keep her harrowing discovery to herself. For years, she silently grappled with the torrent of emotions stirred by her father's murder, burying her pain, anger, and resentment deep within. Then, at the tender age of 16, her body revolted against the weight of her unspoken anguish. Rushed to the hospital amidst crippling chest pain, Candice faced a sobering diagnosis. 'Your body is killing you.' The doctor revealed, 'You weren't having a heart attack, but in my over 20-something years of experience, I have never seen stress symptoms so severe in someone your age.' The severity of her stress symptoms painted a dire picture of her internal turmoil. It was a wake-up call of the gravest kind.

Determined to reclaim her health and well-being, Candice embarked on a relentless quest for healing. She recognized that the root cause of her physical agony lay in the festering resentment she harboured towards her father's murderer. 'Every time I think of this man,' she confessed, 'it's like he controls me, I get these panic attacks. It's like I'm not in control of my own emotions . . . he already killed my father and now he's killing me too.'*

As humans, our initial reaction to perceived wrongs is often one of retaliation. We seek revenge as a means of coping with injustice. Yet, stories like Candice's remind us of a different truth. They illuminate the destructive toll of holding on to grudges, how mental anguish can manifest physically, and the profound benefits of forgiveness for our well-being and inner peace.

We're all aware of the importance of maintaining good health. Many of us consciously engage in activities such as exercise, healthy eating, and meditation to nurture our physical and mental well-being. However, what's truly intriguing is discovering that the path to improved health can sometimes emerge from unexpected sources—even as simple as the act of forgiveness. Simply put, if we want peace, then we have to *choose* to let go. However, the tricky part is that forgiveness doesn't come easy.

Recall a moment when someone treated you unfairly or wronged you. How did you feel and respond? When we're wronged, it's natural to feel hurt and to desire revenge. But whether retaliation is always the solution depends on what we truly seek. Do we crave justice, or do we yearn for inner peace and happiness? Initially, our instinct is often

---

* 'I hugged the man who murdered my father.'. *BBC*, https://tinyurl.com/37k5ptk9 (accessed 12 November 2024).

to pursue justice—to believe that if someone has wronged us, they should face the consequences. However, upon closer reflection, we must ask ourselves: does wishing suffering upon others truly reduce our own pain? In many cases, clinging to bitterness and holding on to grudges only perpetuate our suffering. Despite the event being in the past, our resentment keeps the wounds fresh. So, why wish pain upon another if such an attitude ultimately prolongs our own suffering? Wouldn't it be wiser to respond in a manner that brings us peace even when we're wronged?

Forgiveness is the path to acceptance and inner peace. Although the man responsible for Candice's father's death may not have seemed deserving of forgiveness, for Candice, it became essential. It was her way of seizing control over her circumstances, prioritizing her health, and nurturing her well-being. Forgiveness doesn't justify wrongdoing, nor does it mean subjecting ourselves to further harm; it's a process of healing. When we nurture bitterness, the task of forgiveness becomes increasingly daunting. It's like holding a glass of water in our hand. Initially, the weight may seem negligible, but as time passes, the burden grows heavier and heavier.

Indeed, forgiving can be a monumental challenge, particularly when we're consumed by hurt and the desire for revenge. Yet, figures like Nelson Mandela offer a profound perspective on forgiveness. Mandela, who endured 27 years of imprisonment, approached forgiveness from a place of strength rather than weakness. He famously articulated, 'As I walked out the door toward the gate that would lead to my freedom, I knew that if I didn't leave my bitterness and hatred behind, I'd still be in prison.'*

Moreover, if we acknowledge that everything unfolds according to a higher plan, such as God's will, then we understand that even the wrongs committed against us serve a purpose, ultimately contributing to our growth and development. When viewed through this perspective, the idea of seeking revenge loses its relevance and validity.

A powerful incident from the life of Pramukh Swami Maharaj often resonates with me, exemplifying this attitude in a profound way. In 1986, while recovering from a surgical procedure in Mumbai, a cabinet minister and member of the Planning Commission of India visited him.[†] Despite facing health challenges, Swamiji welcomed the minister, who instead of inquiring about Swamiji's health, chose to instantly insult him. The minister angrily registered his displeasure at the idea of initiating educated young adults as swamis. Throughout the ordeal, Pramukh Swami Maharaj calmly listened, refusing to interrupt or retaliate. He instructed a senior swami not to intervene and insisted that the minister be allowed to speak freely.

When the minister finally exhausted himself after an hour, Swamiji, without a trace of bitterness, glanced at the wall clock, noting it was lunchtime. He then instructed the senior swami to arrange lunch for the minister and his

---

* *Goodreads*, https://tinyurl.com/35m36hms (accessed 11 November 2024).
† Name omitted for anonymity

three accompanying guests. Despite enduring insults while unwell, Swamiji patiently listened to the minister's opinions and extended exceptional hospitality, ensuring the comfort of his visitors throughout their visit.

Two years later, in 1988, Pramukh Swami Maharaj found himself in Nairobi amidst celebrations for his 68th birthday. Around the same time, the minister was also visiting the country for a charity fundraiser. Although he no longer held his seat on the Cabinet and Planning Commission, he was hoping for an opportunity to promote awareness around his charitable initiative at the BAPS festival.

Amidst the stage guests of Kenyan dignitaries, Swamiji did something unusual. Before a crowd of over 5,000, he spotted the ex-minister from a distance, invited him on stage, and then acknowledged him as a respected social worker and former Indian minister. Seating him beside himself, Swamiji personally endorsed the man's fundraising efforts in his address for the night. Moved by this unexpected gesture, the man was overcome with emotion. He recognized Swamiji's kindness, even after the insult. For Pramukh Swami Maharaj, forgiveness wasn't merely about releasing grudges; it was about opening one's heart.

In 2018, we celebrated Pramukh Swami Maharaj's 98th birthday anniversary in Rajkot, under the leadership of Mahant Swami Maharaj. The festival emphasized Pramukh Swami Maharaj's enduring messages on family values, pure living, civic responsibility, nation-building, and women empowerment. The creation of the mini-township relied heavily on the support of local farmers who generously lent their land for the event. While the majority of farmers extended their heartfelt support, a few declined to participate.

On 13 December 2018, amidst the festival's hustle and bustle, Apurvamuni Swami approached Mahant Swami Maharaj with a heartwarming update. He explained how, in adherence to Mahant Swami's guidance, the festival organizers had extended invitations not only to supporters, but also to those who had withheld their backing. To everyone's surprise, those who had initially declined were deeply touched to receive an invitation from Mahant Swami himself. They were given a guided tour of the festival grounds, exploring its shows, exhibitions, and teachings. As instructed by Swamiji, a lavish meal awaited them, served with utmost care and respect. Moved by the gesture, the farmers expressed regret for not offering their land and support. They realized the missed opportunity and also were pleasantly surprised by the profound kindness extended to them despite their initial reluctance.

In response to their heartfelt remorse, Mahant Swami Maharaj offered a profound perspective, stating, 'They accepted our invitation and meal. For me, that is their support.' In this simple yet powerful act of inclusion and compassion, Mahant Swami Maharaj focused solely on the positives, no matter how seemingly trivial.

Let's embrace a similar approach in our daily lives. Can we uncover the positive amidst the negative? Are we willing to let go and heal? Can we transcend our personal hurt for the greater good? Today, take a moment to reflect on any grudges or hurt you may be carrying. Whether it's someone you've distanced yourself from or a pain you've kept buried inside, consider gathering the courage to reach out. Simply saying, 'It's been a long time, let's meet,' can be transformative. Trust me, it will be a moment you'll cherish at the end of your life.

SPIRITUALITY

JUST-IN-TIME WISDOM

'I hear and I forget, I see and I remember, I do and I know.' This timeless proverb holds an important truth. In an era overflowing with information, we enjoy unprecedented access to knowledge from around the world. Yet, we often struggle to translate this knowledge into meaningful action. True wisdom, it appears, isn't merely acquired, but rather mastered through a powerful daily habit.

Yogiji Maharaj often narrated the story of a prince and a minister's son, who shared a deep friendship. Together, they often ventured into the depths of the forests. One fateful night, weary from their travels, they decided to rest beneath the starry night sky. As dawn broke, hunger gnawed at them like never before. In response, the minister's son set out to find food. Upon reaching the forest's edge, he stumbled upon a small town, recently struck by tragedy. With the passing of the ruling king, the town clung to a peculiar tradition: the first person to enter the town on the morning of the ruler's demise would inherit the throne. Thus, when the minister's son crossed the town gates, the subjects declared, 'We have found our new king! The new king is here!'

Meanwhile, back in the forest, the prince, hungry and impatient, sought to discover why his friend had not returned. After a short walk, he arrived at the town gates, and wandering through the market, he stumbled upon a shop adorned with an unusual sign: 'Wisdom Sold Here'. Intrigued, he entered and asked, 'How much for wisdom?' The shopkeeper, with a knowing smile, replied, 'We offer wisdom in various forms, ranging from one rupee to one lakh rupees. The choice is yours.' Without hesitation, the prince traded his precious ring. 'I'll take the one lakh edition,' he declared.

To his astonishment, the shopkeeper retrieved a slip of paper from his pocket and penned a profound message: 'If someone smaller than you is honoured with status, you should kneel before that individual.' Perplexed and perturbed, the prince departed, feeling as though his precious ring had been squandered on a mere piece of paper.

Upon stepping out of the shop, the prince's gaze was drawn to a distant commotion in the streets. As he strained his eyes, he discerned the grand spectacle of a coronation procession unfolding. Squinting further, he realized with a jolt that the figure being elevated to kingship atop an elephant was none other than his companion, the minister's son. Instantly, the prince's initial reaction was one of rage.

'Why him?' he fumed inwardly. 'I, as his senior, deserve this honour. After all, he's merely the son of a minister!'

Yet, in that moment of simmering resentment, the slip of paper in his pocket fluttered to his mind's forefront. Retrieving it, he read the message again: 'If someone smaller than you is honoured with status, you should kneel before that individual.' Suddenly, clarity dawned upon him.

Observing his dear friend adorned in royal attire, the prince humbled himself, sinking to his knees in respect. As the procession drew nearer, the minister's son, now crowned as king, caught sight of his friend's reverent gesture. Halting the procession in its tracks, he insisted that the prince be lifted onto the elephant beside him. With resolve, he declared, 'This friend of mine is not just a companion; he is a prince, destined to be king. Let him be the king, and I will remain his minister!'

Wisdom, or perhaps we could say 'just-in-time wisdom', played a pivotal role in the prince's life. Initially, when he exchanged his precious ring for the slip of paper, he gave little thought to the words inscribed on it. However, when faced with a potential life-and-death situation, the significance of wisdom became glaringly apparent. In that critical moment, he recalled the value of humility and so avoided potential conflict. Moreover, this act of humility not only averted the crisis, but also strengthened the bond with his friend. The prince unlocked an opportunity that might otherwise have remained out of reach. This story portrays the profound impact of timely wisdom in shaping one's path.

We often dedicate significant time and energy to satisfying our thirst for knowledge, whether it be devouring the latest bestseller or subscribing to numerous podcasts. Yet, do we truly recognize the practical value of that knowledge? It's ironic that despite our innate drive to acquire knowledge, we often struggle to integrate it into our daily lives. However, as demonstrated by the prince's experience, wisdom, though simple, possesses a remarkable ability to manifest when needed. It stands distinct from mere knowledge, serving as a valuable asset, readily available for utilization whenever the situation calls for it.

Daily wisdom takes on various forms, tailored to individual preferences and practices. Some seek it through prayer or guidance from revered spiritual gurus, while others absorb teachings from literature, podcasts, or various media platforms. Quote calendars adorning homes and offices are not uncommon. Engaging in daily wisdom often uncovers recurring themes and timeless truths echoed by humanity's profound thinkers across generations. While the sources may vary, the habit of daily exposure to wisdom is a must.

In his primary teachings, compiled in the Vachanamrut, Bhagwan Swaminarayan articulates a practical approach to wisdom. He emphasises that wisdom cannot lead to realization without reflecting on what one has heard or read. Merely acquiring wisdom without deeper reflection serves little purpose.* '[Only] that which is understood clearly is

---

* Sahajananda, Swami. 2014. *The Vachanamrut: Spiritual Discourses of Bhagwan Swaminarayan*. Section Sarangpur 3. Contributors: BAPS, Swaminarayan Aksharpith (2nd ed.).

beneficial—whether it be understood through one verse, or through a hundred verses, or even a thousand verses.'* It's not how much information or wisdom you take in; it's what you do with it that is important.

Expanding on this principle, Bhagwan Swaminarayan shares a pragmatic exercise. He distinguishes between the intake of information, termed as 'shravan', and the discernment of personally relevant insights, known as 'manan'.† In an age bombarded with information from all directions, it's crucial to filter out what is meaningful to us individually. It's not about consuming entire books or podcast episodes in one go; rather, it involves taking time to pause, reflect, and consider what truly resonates with us. By incorporating these moments of reflection into our daily routines, we can effectively internalize this wisdom and apply it to our lives.

When you next reach for a book, consider doing so in the early morning. At this time, your mind tends to be clearer, free from the distractions of the day. As you read through the pages, take it leisurely. Absorb a few pages or a single chapter at a time, and then pause to reflect. If you encounter a moment of inspiration—a spark of awe or wonder—don't rush ahead. Instead, savour it. Allow the

---

* Sahajananda, Swami. 2014. *The Vachanamrut: Spiritual Discourses of Bhagwan Swaminarayan*. Section Sarangpur 4. Contributors: BAPS, Swaminarayan Aksharpith (2nd ed.).

† Sahajananda, Swami. 2014. *The Vachanamrut: Spiritual Discourses of Bhagwan Swaminarayan*. Section Sarangpur 3. Contributors: BAPS, Swaminarayan Aksharpith (2nd ed.).

insight to settle in, cherishing its significance. Visualize how you might apply it throughout the day ahead.

My guru, Mahant Swami Maharaj, stands as a shining example of embracing positive wisdom. From his formative years to the present day, he has immersed himself in diverse literature. Even now, after more than eight decades, he effortlessly draws upon proverbs, poetry, and lessons gleaned from his schooling, as well as the wisdom of eminent leaders and thinkers. Even at the venerable age of 91, he diligently revisits his favourite sacred texts, pausing to reflect, sometimes noting his insights in journals. When inspired, he immerses himself in profound contemplation, sometimes devoting hours or even days to internalizing a single proverb. This genuine approach allows him to effortlessly share experiential wisdom to the masses, not as rehearsed speeches, but as living truths applicable to daily life—a testament to spiritual maturity.

On 5 September 2017, Mahant Swami Maharaj met former US President, Barack Obama, in Washington D.C.

'I longed to meet you.' Swamiji revealed.

'Why is that, Mahant Swami?' Obama asked.

'You are humble, that is why.'

Drawing inspiration from more than 70 years ago, Swamiji recited a poem he had learnt in school and had etched into his daily life:

He that is down need fear no fall,
He that is low no pride.
He that is humble ever shall
Have God to be his guide.

While school rhymes may seem simple, when combined with a commitment to internalize their lessons, they can be truly transformative. We must create a habit to engage with daily wisdom. Then, pause and reflect. Again, and again. Consistently engaging with wisdom will offer invaluable insights, clarity, and most crucially, readiness during those critical times. We must take the first step. Let's commit to the regular habit of internalizing inspiration and keeping those slips of just-in-time wisdom readily available throughout the day.

DAILY REFLECTION

My guru, Mahant Swami Maharaj, often emphasizes the urgent need for self-reflection in our journeys: 'How are we internally? Who are we? What is it that we need to do? What is it that we are doing currently? We should try to answer these questions for ourselves daily. Otherwise, years will pass us by, and we may not accomplish anything of substance.'

Once, I explored the story of a pious man from the 19th century. His life unfolded in the culturally vibrant city of Junagadh, which is situated in the western part of the Indian state of Gujarat. Despite being well-regarded in the community, his frequent angry outbursts at home often obscured the love he had for his family. If a meal fell short of his expectations, a fit of anger would engulf his home, leaving his family perpetually on edge.

In search of solace, the man's family turned to Gunatitanand Swami Maharaj, the wise chief swami of their local Swaminarayan temple. Swami encouraged the man to participate in daily assemblies, where he shared wisdom about genuine devotion, personal growth, and life's ultimate goals. Intrigued, the man found himself increasingly drawn to Swami's talks.

As time elapsed, curiosity about Swami's life gripped him. The man was aware that mandirs traditionally offered sumptuous food to the images of God as acts of devotion. He, thus, presumed Swami himself would succumb to the allure of these rich and sweet delicacies. As he peeked into the dining area, he discovered Swami sitting cross-legged on the floor and partaking in a bland meal of whole-grain roti and diluted yogurt from a simple wooden bowl. It became evident that the chief swami had willingly set aside the indulgence of his taste buds, opting instead for a diet common among the village folk.

The stark contrast compelled the man to reevaluate his preconceptions. As the clouds of misunderstanding slowly dissipated, a deeper clarity about himself emerged. Strolling homeward, he started to reflect on the consequences of his behaviour. He began to recognize the disparity between his unrealistic expectations and the person he aspired to be. He contemplated the toll his short temper took on his loved ones and pondered on the simplicity of Swami's eating habits.

Upon returning home late that day, the man was hesitantly served a cold meal by his wife. She was expecting to hear bitter words of resentment, but to her surprise, her husband consumed the food without a single complaint. Meal by meal, day by day, he discarded expectations and grievances. His insatiable taste gave way to contentment and kind words, fostering a newfound intimacy within his family. His once tumultuous home transformed into a haven of peace. One profound moment of self-reflection became the catalyst for personal growth, ushering in a more harmonious family life with tranquility.

This age-old incident involving a man from Junagadh remains remarkably relevant in today's context. Amid the overwhelming pressures of our responsibilities, it is easy to become stressed, reactive, and unmindful. Regrettably, as time passes, this burden can potentially erode our character and adversely affect those we hold dear. This behaviour indicates a misalignment between our values, beliefs, and goals as well as the way we navigate our daily lives. Routine introspection can ensure we stay within our envisioned ideals.

Dedicating even a few minutes each day to reflect on our spiritual journey and realigning our internal compass with the external world can bring significant benefits to our well-being and development. Bhagwan Swaminarayan likened this daily self-reflection to the habits of an astute businessman. He explained that a successful businessman diligently checks his accounts every day to ascertain whether his efforts have been profitable.* Similarly, in life, true progress and goal achievement only reveal themselves through regular self-reflection.

---

* Sahajananda, Swami. 2014. *The Vachanamrut: Spiritual Discourses of Bhagwan Swaminarayan*. Section Gadhada I 38, Contributors: Bochasanvasi Shri Aksharpurushottama Sanstha, Swaminarayan Aksharpith (2nd ed.). Ahmedabad.

The holistic health and wellness expert, Dr Sukhraj Dhillon, aptly remarked, 'You should sit in meditation for 20 minutes every day—unless you're too busy. Then you should sit for one hour.' This insight does not necessarily seek to emphasize the duration of reflection, but the crucial act of dedicating daily time to it. The notion that one cannot spare even 20 minutes hints at a lack of clarity in priorities and self-neglect. Ironically, those who relentlessly dedicate every waking minute to their work may be the ones in dire need of reflection. It is in the quiet moments of each day that a profound understanding of our inner selves can be gained. Though brief, those moments of stillness pave the way for personal growth and enhance productivity toward our long-term goals.

While there are numerous methods for conducting self-reflection, allow me to share a few that have proven particularly beneficial for me:

1. **Meditation**:

   Hindu wisdom offers various paths to spiritual growth, each catering to the diverse nature of individuals. One method is meditation, a practice that helps the mind transcend limitations and connect with the Divine. There are a variety of manners in which one can meditate. One of the most popular includes 'jap' meditation, where the practitioner closes one's eyes and silently or audibly recites a mantra such as 'Aum Namah Shivaya' or 'Swaminarayan' while remaining focussed on the Divine. Bringing stillness to one's mind through meditation creates an effective mental environment for self-reflection.

2. Journaling:

Keep a daily journal where you write about your thoughts, experiences, and emotions. Reflect on your day, noting what went well, what could have been better, and how you could go about improving. Ask yourself open-ended questions about your goals, values, and priorities. Examples include: 'What am I grateful for today?' or 'What can I do differently tomorrow to achieve my goals?'

3. Self-Questioning:

The Satsang Diksha is a sacred text written by Mahant Swami Maharaj based on the teachings of Bhagwan Swaminarayan. This text concisely describes philosophical principles with practical application. In the Satsang Diksha, verse 145, Mahant Swami Maharaj instructs, 'With a composed mind, one should introspect daily: "What have I come to accomplish in this world, and what am I doing?"' This provides a coherent and practical way to start each day. It involves reinforcing one's life purpose by comparing it to one's daily actions.

Equipped with these methods in our toolkit, we can reap a multitude of benefits from self-reflection. It amplifies self-awareness, strengthens our beliefs and values, provides clarity on goals, enhances emotional intelligence, refines decision-making, alleviates stress, nurtures heightened gratitude, and connects us with the Divine. So let us learn to embrace each day by taking heed of the wisdom shared by Socrates: 'An unexamined life is not worth living.'

WHAT CAN I GIVE?

In a world where self-centredness often prevails, we find some remarkable individuals proactively prioritize the well-being of others above themselves. By exploring the stories of two legends, a national president and a revered spiritual leader, who won the hearts of millions, we too can bring a positive change to the world.

Imagine yourself standing in a queue at a bustling supermarket, your body weary and your shopping cart brimming with groceries. Behind you, a frazzled lady attempts to soothe her restless toddler, the strains of her efforts evident in her eyes. Alternatively, picture yourself stepping onto a plane, eager to settle into your window seat, only to discover a curious teenager occupying your reserved spot, their eyes filled with awe and curiosity. Alternatively, envision yourself hurrying down a crowded pavement when you catch sight of an elderly stranger struggling to navigate her smartphone, her frustration palpable.

In such moments, the choices we make define our character. How would you react? Would you prioritize your own needs or extend a helping hand to those around you, however inconvenienced you may be?

We all have our own stories, instances where we've brightened someone's day through a simple act of kindness or unintentionally overlooked someone due to the pressures of our own lives. However, what sets legendary personalities apart is their proactive approach to helping others. They don't wait to be asked for assistance; they actively seek out opportunities to make a difference in the lives of strangers. Their existence is fuelled by the desire to bring joy to the faces of others, consistently placing the needs of others above their own. And in doing so, they become beacons of inspiration, encouraging those around them to embrace a similar selfless mindset.

Former President of India, Dr A.P.J. Abdul Kalam, embodied humility and a commitment to public service, serving as an inspiration to millions. His remarkable qualities were evident in various encounters.

During a demanding project where Dr Kalam held the position of programme director, one of the 70 scientists working under him approached him with a request. The scientist had promised his children that he would take them to an exhibition and asked if he could leave at 5.30 p.m. Dr Kalam permitted him without hesitation. However, engrossed in his work, the scientist lost track of time and realized he was late only at 8.30 p.m. Overwhelmed with guilt for disappointing his kids, he hurried home, only to discover that Dr Kalam had arrived at 5.15 p.m. and taken the children to the exhibition himself.

Dr Kalam had noticed the scientist's dedication at 5 p.m. and correctly anticipated his commitment to work. However, understanding the importance of fulfilling promises made to loved ones, Dr Kalam selflessly took the initiative to ensure the children could enjoy the exhibition. This act of kindness and consideration revealed his leadership and caring nature.

Mandira S. Lalvani, a sports presenter, had an unforgettable encounter with Dr A.P.J. Abdul Kalam during a flight from Dehradun to Delhi. By chance, she found herself occupying his assigned seat on an ATR domestic flight, while her own seat was in the non-reclining last row. As Dr Kalam boarded the flight at the last minute, his security detail requested Mandira to vacate the seat. However, Dr Kalam personally approached her, offering his apologies on behalf of his security team and insisting that she remain in that seat. Mandira was deeply impressed by his graciousness and considered him a true gentleman.

Another remarkable incident involving Dr Kalam took place during a journey to IIM Shillong. Accompanied by Srijan Pal Singh, an education innovator and advisor, Dr Kalam expressed concern about a soldier standing atop an open SUV in their convoy. He requested a wireless message be sent for the soldier to sit, but Singh explained the need for enhanced security. Dr Kalam persisted, reminding Singh throughout the journey to signal the soldier to sit. Despite the security protocol, Dr Kalam's empathy and respect for the soldier's well-being were unwavering. Upon reaching their destination, Singh located the soldier and brought him to Dr Kalam. The former President greeted the soldier warmly, shook his hand, and apologized for the prolonged standing. The young guard, astonished by the unexpected gesture, found himself momentarily overwhelmed, struggling to find the right words. Finally, he managed to express his admiration, declaring, 'Sir, for you, we would willingly stand for six hours and more.'

These instances, of Dr Kalam's compassion and concern for others endeared him to the public, earning him the well-deserved title of the 'People's President'.

Pramukh Swami Maharaj, too, exemplified selflessness and humility in various situations. On one occasion, during preparations for a grand celebration in Vadodara in 1965, a truck loaded with mattresses arrived at around 1.30 a.m. The truck driver wanted to leave straight away, so the mattresses had to be unloaded. Apart from Pramukh Swami Maharaj and another swami, everyone else was fast asleep.

The fellow swami was about to wake up some youths to get help unloading the truck. But Swamiji said, 'No, they've performed seva all day and must be tired. I will stand here, you get onto the truck and pass me the mattresses. I will stack them in the corner.'

Together they completed this long, repetitive, and strenuous task until 3.00 a.m. It would have been done much quicker with the help of the youths. However, Swamiji cared more about them being fully rested rather than his own body and fatigue.

In 2001, immediately after the Gujarat earthquake, Pramukh Swami Maharaj sent a group of swamis to lead the BAPS disaster relief efforts. I was fortunate to be a part of that team. Initially, we set up hot meals for 17,000 victims in Bhuj. Over the next six to eight months, BAPS teams set up relief kitchens to feed hot meals to more than 1.2 million victims and volunteers, and provided free medical care to 91,000 people. To reach victims in remote areas, Swamiji also directed the production and distribution of relief kits to a lot of villages.*

While serving the victims, I collaborated with Mr Shalom, the head of the Israeli disaster relief team. Intrigued by the scale of hot meals served in the relief kitchens, he initiated a detailed discussion about BAPS's efforts. The conversation soon turned to the contents of the relief packages. 'Alongside the standard items, we also include a nail cutter, a comb, and a bottle of oil,' I explained.

'Why these items?' Mr. Shalom questioned.

'My guru, Pramukh Swami Maharaj, insisted,' I explained. 'It's been quite a few days since the earthquake, so they may need to cut their nails to feel comfortable while eating. And with limited access to bathing water due to the earthquake, a comb and hair oil can help them freshen up.'

'Can I see his picture?' he requested. As I handed him Swamiji's photo, he squinted his eyes, studying it closely

---

* BAPS. November 2022. *A Story of Struggle and Restoration.* 4-Part Documentary Series—the 2001 Gujarat Earthquake. *BAPS*, https://tinyurl.com/mr44vd8z (accessed 12 November 2024).

before asking, 'From which university did he study his MBA?'

'He hasn't studied an MBA. He completed only his primary education in a village in Gujarat.'

Mr Shalom paused for a moment and then shared his thoughts. 'We have many long and detailed meetings on how to handle natural disasters and our first response. But we've never come across these ideas. Pramukh Swami has such unique thoughts to help people. The difference is we work from the brain, and he works from the heart.'

Once at the BAPS Swaminarayan Mandir in Ahmedabad, Dr Kalam was asked to divulge the source of his unwavering energy, enthusiasm, and positivity. To this, he gave a startling reply. 'I learned this secret from Pramukh Swamiji . . . wherever I go, whatever I do, whomever I meet, I only ask one question: What can I give? What can I give? What can I give?'

This simple yet powerful mantra encapsulates Dr Kalam's and Pramukh Swami Maharaj's selfless outlook and relentless commitment to serving others. If we were all to embrace this mantra as our own, the collective impact would truly make our world an amazing place.

LIVE EACH DAY AS IF IT WERE YOUR LAST

S teve Jobs once said, 'Remembering that I will be dead soon is the most important tool I've ever encountered to help me make the big choices in life. Remembering that you are going to die is the best way I know to avoid the trap of thinking you have something to lose. You are already naked. There is no reason not to follow your heart.'*

In the Hindu epic known as the Mahabharat, Yudhishthir is posed a cryptic question, 'What is the greatest wonder of this world?' Intriguingly, Yudhishthir didn't respond by describing grand palaces or natural phenomena. Instead, he revealed a subtle phenomenon of the human psyche, 'Although, before our very eyes, we witness people

---

* 24 August 2022. '"You've got to find what you love," Jobs says.' *Stanford News*, https://tinyurl.com/44bfba4u (accessed 11 November 2024).

perishing and dying at every moment of every day, we never, for once, feel that death shall also befall us in the same way.' This answer encapsulates a truth to which we can all relate. Most of us wouldn't have contemplated death too deeply, and why would we? Nothing in our current culture suggests we keep death at the forefront of our lives. When we are young, we have no reason to ponder over it. As we grow older, we think about it more frequently, but for the most part, it remains a subject mostly avoided.

While we readily accept the inevitability of death as a fact, it is worthwhile to pause and reflect upon the profound magnitude that death holds. The world as you know it is constructed from your experiences. Reflect on your childhood, your first day of school, the picture on your bedroom wall, your tenth birthday party, favourite memories with your parents, instances of trauma, old toys, favourite TV shows, vacations, and school friends. Consider how you've grown, tracing your experiences to the present day. Recognize the areas of your relationships that have shaped your current behaviour. From struggles in college to obtaining your degree, securing a job, and having children, all of this has shaped your unique world, influencing your thoughts, behaviour, and priorities.

Now, for a moment, ponder over the harsh reality that all of this will one day disappear. Everything you've strived for—your possessions, wealth, and prestige—will cease to exist. Your friends, family, and children will vanish along with your world. Your story in this world will remain largely untold, with little significance. Those who remember your name or face will eventually pass away, and the final traces of your presence will vanish.

Although there is always a part of our minds that knows we won't be here forever, we frequently overlook the profound significance of this inevitable reality. If our bodies cannot accompany us after death, then from where does the question of our possessions arise? People spend their entire lives accumulating more and more, only to leave it all behind. We toil tirelessly in a continuous routine until our bodies give up. Towards the end, we may have much of what we desired, but our bodies are often worn out, limiting our ability to enjoy what we have accumulated over a lifetime. We sit there, weary and tired, waiting for our children to visit. Can you honestly say that you will be content then?

It's a daunting idea to consider, which is why most prefer to avoid thinking about it. However, death teaches us about life. It empowers us to embrace each day as if it were our last. Don't get me wrong; we need both short and long-term goals. Planning a career, achieving financial security, and supporting family and friends are essential responsibilities. Death is not an excuse to neglect these responsibilities, but it provides us with the wisdom to embrace our ultimate goals. Death offers clarity about what truly matters as well as a sense of urgency to prioritize accordingly.

In the late 1960s to 1970s, Steve McQueen, a Hollywood star, gained fame for his rebellious style and on-screen charisma, earning him the title 'The King of Cool'. Performing his own stunts and receiving numerous award nominations for Best Actor, he upheld a proud and resolute demeanour, securing a prominent position at the top of the charts. That was until, at the age of 42, the doctors signed him off as a patient of terminal cancer. When the reality of death stared him in the face, fear struck. He struggled to play a role he hadn't played before. Now, with his career on the line and dreams shattering, he became desperate. But how could such a star put his ego aside and seek help? What would happen to his past successes and publicity built upon until now? He soon realized that to reach a state of inner peace and acceptance, he had to put his painful ego aside. He did this by turning towards spirituality, saying in his own words, 'I have touched God. He has given me more courage than I have ever had in my life.' Unfortunately, McQueen never recovered, but he died a different death. Throughout his life, he had indulged in fame and wealth, yet on the brink of death, these pursuits amounted to nothing. This awakening allowed him to pursue a more meaningful purpose, one that could bring him peace.

For nine decades, Pramukh Swami Maharaj consistently emphasized the reality of death. I recall him explaining, 'Everything is perishable; one day, everything, including each one of us, will perish and be destroyed. Constantly remain aware of this fact.' The noteworthy term here is 'constant awareness'—not merely a consideration for the end, but a daily tool for reflection. Swamiji consistently imparted this wisdom, appreciating not only its capacity to bring clarity, but also its potent ability to offer strength and stability, particularly during challenging times.

26 January 2001 was a day that shook the nation of India. An earthquake that lasted for only two minutes went on to cause damage that lasted for years, and for some, a lifetime. With a magnitude of 6.9 on the Richter scale, it was described as the most devastating earthquake in the past 150 years. The earthquake left the city of Bhuj, in Gujarat, and its surrounding areas in ruins. It took the lives of over 20,000 people and injured more than 150,000. Kalpesh Bhatt, now an assistant professor at the University of Mary Washington, was volunteering in Bhuj at the time. He first-hand witnessed the horrors of the disaster.

Amidst the chaos, Kalpesh noticed an elderly man sitting calmly upon a pile of debris from a collapsed building. He approached the man who seemed to be lost in some thought. Kalpesh kindly offered him some tea and asked him if anyone in his family had been affected by this tragic calamity. The old man mentioned that he was in fact sitting upon everything that was once his—his two-storey home, his wife, his sons, his grandchildren—all of that was now gone. His response left Kalpesh lost for words and visibly upset. Surprisingly, the elderly man started to console him. 'Have you read the [Bhagavad] Gita?' he asked and continued. 'I used to read it daily, believing it would come in use. Today that day has come.' He went on to recall a verse from the Bhagavad Gita (2.27) and explained that anyone who is born is destined to die. Everything is perishable and doesn't last. In five to 10 years, he knew that he too was going to die. And after his death, everything would cease to exist for him. He strongly believed that it was the Divine's wish that the situation had been reversed, 'First they go, and then I will go.' Kalpesh was astounded at the man's ability to remain stable despite such an awful personal experience. The elderly man went on to accompany Kalpesh at a food camp, where he served food to many victims and gave them words of encouragement at such a challenging time.

This understanding has transformed many. Recognizing the finitude of our existence empowers us to prioritize what truly matters. It enables us to stay focussed and perform actions in this world without attachment. Constant awareness of this reality provides the stability and resilience we need to navigate challenges. For death, it seems, is not the bane of life, but a stark reminder to embrace each day.

BALANCED WITHIN

Resilience is crucial for survival, yet true stability extends beyond mere endurance. Navigating life's storms with unruffled composure, standing steadfast in the face of insult, and embracing proactivity amidst pressure are qualities surpassing resilience; they are the hallmarks of inner balance. Genuine stability stems from authentic spirituality, and the journey begins quite simply—with a little extra faith.

On 23 April 2017, Mahant Swami Maharaj descended into Kolkata airspace, greeted not only by the relentless 35°C (95°F) heat but also by a series of unforeseen challenges. The aircraft, graced by clear skies, touched down at Kolkata Airport at 12.15 p.m. After blessing the pilot, Swamiji awaited the vehicle that would take him to the next destination. However, time seemed to stretch as the vehicle arrived late at 2.05 p.m. With almost two hours lost, Swamiji prepared for the next leg of his journey without complaint.

Yet, a series of unexpected setbacks unfolded. The transit assistant, growing increasingly frustrated, engaged in lengthy discussions with authorities. Despite having completed all the required paperwork, they were denied permission to leave. The stifling heat of the unventilated area added to the discomfort, yet Mahant Swami Maharaj, at 83 years old, remained remarkably calm and composed throughout the ordeal.

After another hour of waiting, Swamiji showed visible signs of discomfort from the heat. This alarmed the accompanying swamis, who became concerned for his well-being and appealed to the authorities for permission to exit. Finally, as they drove out the airport, Swamiji expressed his magnanimity with a gentle remark: 'It's not their fault.'

Over the following three days, Mahant Swami Maharaj battled weakness, fever, and vomiting—a testament to the toll the ordeal must have taken on his health. Yet not a single expression of anger or frustration surfaced on Swamiji's face throughout the incident. Intrigued by his calm composure, an accompanying swami finally sought the secret behind Swamiji's patience. In response, Swamishri divulged his profound wisdom, 'Whatever happens is due to the wish of God.'*

Swamishri's response is worth reflecting on. Throughout our daily journey, we encounter a series of highs and lows,

---

* Brahmavatsaldas, Sadhu, and Mahant Prasangamrut. 23 April 2017. *Chronicles of Mahant Swami Maharaj.*

where even the minutest disturbance has the power to unsettle us. Whether it's a road accident disrupting our commute, an inconvenient headache preceding a significant event, or an unpleasant comment on social media, the slightest disruption can cast a shadow over our entire day. While the temptation to react is strong, attempting to combat every minor annoyance is simply a waste of energy. Instead, the wisdom lies in cultivating ourselves. Surely, it's easier to wear shoes than to sweep every thorn and rock from our path.

While many contemporary thinkers offer useful insights to cope with such situations, the lives of spiritual giants unveil an ultimate solution for stability: faith in God. By placing trust in a higher power, one can rise beyond the situation. Yes, the challenges may remain, but their influence is nullified. One can remain immersed yet distinct. Pramukh Swami Maharaj revealed this process through a metaphor: 'You only feel the burden on your head when you attempt to carry a pot of water. Yet when you swim in the ocean, with thousands of gallons of water above your head, you feel nothing. Similarly, you should always pray to God saying, "You are doing everything; I am merely an instrument." He will guide us through both success and failure.'

The Bhagavad Gita (2.47) explains our duty as the performance of karmas—to harbour ambition, envision goals, persevere, and achieve—all while embracing the ultimate acceptance of results as God's divine will. To embody this wisdom demands a journey beyond the confines of mere logic, delving into the profound realm of faith. Though challenging, this endeavour proves immensely potent, perhaps appearing abstract at first yet yielding tangible and rewarding outcomes. This practical embodiment of faith unfolded vividly in the life of Pramukh Swami Maharaj, providing a living testament to its power.

In 1968, Pramukh Swami Maharaj's revered guru, Yogiji Maharaj, envisioned a magnificent mandir on the serene banks of the River Yamuna in New Delhi. However, the realization of this vision was a testament to patience and endurance, taking a staggering 32 years to acquire the land. Along this arduous journey, marked by apparent setbacks, legal intricacies, and unfounded opposition, Pramukh Swami Maharaj's unflinching faith in God emerged as the driving force behind his resilience, optimism, and magnanimity.

On 8 November 2000, with the long-awaited permissions secured, the construction of the project commenced. However, the path ahead was fraught with immense challenges—logistical complications, sparse resources, and an overwhelming workload. The task at hand was daunting: 6,000 tonnes of pink sandstone needed to be intricately carved by 7,000 artisans across Rajasthan. Every night, over 100 trucks transported these crafted stones to the construction site in Delhi, where 4,000 volunteers would slot the pieces together, much like a colossal puzzle. The goal was nothing short of ambitious: construct one of the world's largest temples in under five years!

Amidst the construction site, where stones scattered the horizon, a skeptical team member couldn't help but voice his doubt: 'No external company would ever dare to take on a project of this magnitude, considering the arbitrary schedule and proposed deadline. Can't you feel the weight of these gigantic stones?'

In response, Pramukh Swami Maharaj unveiled the depth of his faith, 'There can be thousands of stones up there. However, I don't feel even the weight of a pebble on my chest.'

Taking just two days less than five years to complete, the now-completed BAPS Swaminarayan Akshardham proudly adorned the city of Delhi on 6 November 2005. Upon entering the complex, the Indian president, prime minister, and leader of the opposition marvelled at the monument's expression of India's pride, culture, values, and wisdom. Swamiji's ability to empower and unify thousands of volunteers and artisans earned him widespread praise. However, amid universal acclaim, his response remained consistent, sincere, and humble: 'It is only possible due to the grace of God.'

From the lows of setbacks, opposition, and heavy workloads to the highs of honour and praise, Pramukh Swami Maharaj stood graciously grounded and blissfully unburdened. His secret lay in his unflinching faith in God. When life's burdens weigh us down, let's resist succumbing to impulsive reactions and reluctant restraint. Rather than relying solely on our resilience, let's draw inspiration from the lives of spiritual giants. Why burden ourselves when, perhaps, all we truly need is a little extra faith?

BEYOND THE BODY

'Who am I?' This question is not only profound but impacts our daily lives. It guides us to a better understanding of ourselves, imbues actions with purpose, and empowers us to redefine our circumstances. Yet, above all, this journey of self-discovery holds the transformative power to shape our very existence.

In the ancient land of India, the Mahabharat recounts a remarkable tale about a boy. He was born with deformities in eight places on his body, a condition that tragically earned him the name Ashtavakra, meaning 'bent in eight places'. Regrettably, his disability subjected him to scorn and ridicule from many. Nevertheless, Ashtavakra exhibited an extraordinary sense of self-confidence, security, and inner strength.

As he neared the age of 12, a troubling truth emerged: his father had been defeated in a debate by the renowned Varani and faced punishment by drowning. Faced with this tragic revelation, Ashtavakra resolved to restore his father's honour. Despite his young age, Ashtavakra fearlessly embarked on a quest to challenge Varani to a debate.

Ashtavakra attempted to enter the royal court, but the guards denied him entry on learning his age. They doubted someone so young could qualify for a scholarly platform. Unfazed, Ashtavakra challenged their perception of age. 'A grey head does not make an elder,' he masterfully declared. 'Not by years, not by grey hairs, not by riches nor by relations did the seers make the Law. He who is great to us is one who has learning.'* Stunned upon hearing such insight, the guards allowed him entry.

Upon entering the royal court, Ashtavakra encountered scorn and discrimination once more, this time from Varani. Undeterred, Ashtavakra maintained his composure and engaged Varani in a spirited challenge. Their ensuing debate unfolded as an extraordinary spectacle, a poetic clash of intellect and wit. Ashtavakra's sharp mind and profound wisdom astonished the audience, leading him to emerge triumphant amidst thunderous cheers from the gathered scholars.

Encountering discrimination based on age, disability, and circumstance, Ashtavakra remained unperturbed. His self-assurance stemmed from a deep understanding that the identity of his body did not determine his true essence. He acknowledged that names and physical appearances clouded

---

* Buitenen, J.A.B., trans. 'Ashtavakra, Vana Parva'. *The Mahabharata, Volume 2*, 1981.

the perception of the ignorant, whereas the wise saw only the essence of one's being.*

Among the spectators that day was King Janak, who observed with curiosity. Initially, he viewed Ashtavakra simply as a boy burdened with deformity. However, as he witnessed the wisdom and strength of Ashtavakra's words, the king's perception was transformed. Recognizing Ashtavakra's excellence, King Janak likened his prowess to that of celestial beings—not merely a mortal or a child, but truly wise.† King Janak soon became Ashtavakra's eager student. The profound lessons he learned left an enduring impact, shaping his self-understanding, treatment of others, and outlook on life.

Throughout his life, Bhagwan Swaminarayan emphasized self-inquiry, recognizing that as long as individuals perceive the body as their true self, their wisdom remains futile. He explained that we are not the body or mind, but rather the 'jiva', a Sanskrit term meaning 'life-force' or 'that which lives'. We are the 'atma', the spirit, characterized by 'sat-chit-anand', denoting true existence, consciousness, and bliss. Unlike the temporary and destructible nature of the body, we are eternal enlightened beings with the potential to experience constant bliss. However, we have forgotten who we truly are.

We often define ourselves through our bodies, possessions, and relationships, using terms like 'I' and

---

* 'The birth of Ashtavakra and his entry into the court of Raja Janaka'. *Sandeepa*, https://tinyurl.com/5fxw6sbf (accessed 11 November 2024).
† Ibid.

'mine'. We say, 'This is *my* face', 'These are *my* possessions', and 'These are *my* people'. While our needs for things and relationships are crucial for survival and progress, the concept of 'mine' inherently creates a divide—where there is something that is 'mine', there is something that is 'not yours'. When we claim ownership over '*my* country' and '*my* people' only, we distance ourselves from problems and pain of people of other countries, failing to recognize them as our own. Rooted in this sense of 'I-ness' and 'my-ness', this ingrained belief system creates hurt, division, and selfishness.

To grasp the depth of this dilemma, let's pause to contemplate how we typically construct our identities. Often, we fall into the trap of equating our value with external possessions—our clothes, houses, cars, or the latest gadgets we own. Society, too, tends to categorize us based on our wealth and social standing, confining us within a narrow framework that stifles our true potential.

Moreover, when we gaze into the mirror, we might find ourselves scrutinizing our physical appearance—the flaws, imperfections, and the relentless pursuit of an idealized image. Unwittingly, we may allow our insecurities, whether related to age, weight, height, skin, or intelligence, to define us. When judged negatively by these attributes, it's natural to feel hurt and anxious. This occurs because we allow these bodily characteristics to shape our identities and dictate our happiness.

What about the darker aspects of our personalities, the traits that often hinder our progress—like a short temper, easy irritability, jealousy, stubbornness, self-centredness, or negativity? Do we permit these flaws to define us, to control the narrative of our lives? Understanding the concept of the jiva urges us to transcend these limitations, to realize that they don't represent the core of our being, but rather distinct facets that we can acknowledge, accept, and improve upon. We aren't defined by our flaws; rather, we're defined by our ability to rise above them, nurture greater self-awareness, and embrace the higher aspects of our nature.

However, it's important to note that embracing our identity as the jiva does not diminish the importance of physical health, talent development, or education. On the contrary, the Bhagavad Gita encourages us to fulfil such responsibilities. The distinction lies in recognizing that these external aspects do not define our essence. They act as vehicles for navigating the world, fostering personal growth, and spiritual maturity.

The influence of 'I-ness' extends beyond individual suffering to affect the world on a larger scale. Ignorance fosters superficial perspectives and unjust stereotypes, hindering personal development. Ego drives conflict, impedes empathy, and disrupts relationships, leading to fractures in families, friendships, and professional collaborations. It fuels social prejudice, political discord, and environmental neglect, contributing to conflicts ranging from domestic disputes to global wars, perpetuating a cycle of suffering throughout history.

The relentless pursuit to transcend ignorance constitutes a central objective in nearly every Hindu school of thought.

Termed as 'mukti' or 'moksha', derived from the Sanskrit root 'much' meaning 'to become free', this concept denotes liberation. Bhagwan Swaminarayan reveals the ultimate goal, or mukti, for jivas is to attain liberation from the constraints of ignorance and offer ultimate devotion to Parabrahma, the supreme. Through mukti, we possess the potential to experience stability, enlightenment, unburdened existence, and divine bliss. However, the question remains: how do we achieve this?

Bhagwan Swaminarayan advocated seeking guidance from enlightened mentors—individuals who themselves have achieved mukti. But does such spiritual elevation truly exist? Or is it merely confined to books and discussions? Dr Tejas Patel harboured doubts. As the chairman and chief interventional cardiologist of Apex Heart Institute, Ahmedabad, he was intimately acquainted with the intricacies and ailments of the human body. Having witnessed the pain expressed by thousands of patients, he was acutely aware of the limitations inherent in the human experience. However, one particular incident shifted his perspective.

On 15 June 2012, Dr Patel was tasked with performing a unique procedure. While pacemaker implantation was routine for a cardiologist, the age and health of his patient—Pramukh Swami Maharaj—posed a significant risk. At the age of 90, general anesthesia was deemed too perilous. Dr Patel cautioned Swamiji to brace himself for a 'very painful procedure'. During the incision, tissue separation, and pacemaker implantation, Dr Patel closely monitored Swamiji's condition, regularly inquiring about his comfort and studying his facial expressions. Yet, to Dr Patel's surprise, there were 'no complaints during the procedure . . . or afterwards'. Swamiji remained 'completely calm, quiet, and composed'.

Reflecting on this experience, Dr Patel recalled the wisdom of the Bhagavad Gita, which states 'the soul and body as two separate things'. But he admits his doubts. Wisdom is one thing, he explains, but 'practical experience' is another. Yet while operating on Pramukh Swami Maharaj, he 'experienced and realized' this wisdom firsthand. He felt that Swamiji had 'completely separated his soul from the body. All these external pains, and problems and troubles, they just touched his body and went away'. Dr Patel explained, 'I don't think they touched his soul. He was completely rock steady throughout.'*

Dr Abdul Kalam also sought experiential wisdom throughout his life. As the President of India and a renowned scientist, he interacted with numerous influential thinkers, innovators, and world leaders. However, he believed that it was the guidance of spiritual luminaries that truly transformed him. Renowned as the 'People's President', Dr Kalam embodied humility, generosity, and devotion. Yet, he regarded transcending his 'I-ness' and 'my-ness' as the final piece of his spiritual journey.

'I felt as if through Pramukh Swamiji a divine message was transferred to me about something endowed to mankind

---

* 'Interview with Dr Tejas Patel', *Youtube*, https://tinyurl.com/5n7us9dy (accessed 11 November 2024).

by God Almighty, but forgotten from history.' Dr Kalam explains:

> I realized that the struggle between happiness and unhappiness that had so far been the story of human experience—and the struggle between peace and war has been the history of the human race—must change . . . A harmonious world may seem an impossible utopian vision. But with the guidance of the Divine, and in acknowledging the unity of all creation—and with the helping hand of such transcendent souls as Pramukh Swamiji—the impossible may be achieved. And a harmonious world begins with a harmonious inner world . . . For us to ignite our spirituality, we need to look inward and transcend our ego.*

As we develop a deeper level of self-awareness—aligning our identity with our true selves—we learn to acknowledge suffering without identifying with it. Witnessing the life of Mahant Swami Maharaj, I have experienced first-hand his transcendence and selflessness. Emerging from a car crash with a broken jaw, Swamiji urged doctors to prioritize treating others with lesser injuries. Even when insulted, Swamiji exudes only unconditional compassion. In sickness, his devotion remains heartfelt and unwavering. He has detached himself from the physical and mental suffering of

---

* A.P.J. Abdul Kalam. *Transcendence: My Spiritual Experiences with Pramukh Swamiji*. pp. xii. Harper Element.

this world, experiencing and perceiving nothing but God. Through these trials, Swamiji's life stands as a testament to the possibility of transcending suffering. Such a life becomes a blessing, embodying the spirit of giving, sharing, and caring without any expectations in return.

COSMIC CONVERSATION

Our reality is ever-changing, where joy gives way to sorrow, success to failure, and life to death. It's unpredictable. It's turbulent. It's part of human existence. To cope with uncertainty, we seek security, comfort, and support—yet even these can prove fleeting. Amid the chaos and clamour of the world, a quiet space exists. To find stability, we must look within. It's a connection, a conversation, a constant.

Long ago, there stood a massive three-peaked mountain called Trikuta. It towered over a lush jungle at its base, where a herd of elephants lived. Gajendra, the mighty elephant king, led the herd. Every day, they roamed through the forest, trampling over the land and enjoying the abundance of fruits and other vegetation. While wandering through the trees one day, the herd grew tired and thirsty. Gajendra raised his trunk and sniffed the air, catching the scent of lotuses carried by a breeze from a distant lake. He led the herd as they eagerly stomped through the jungle, heading towards the scent.

When the elephants reached the lake, they trumpeted with joy and rushed into the water. They drank and bathed, splashing about, their exuberance disturbing the once-tranquil surface. But as they enjoyed the cool water, they were unaware of the hidden danger below. Without warning, a massive crocodile surged from the depths, its eyes burning with rage and its jaws stretched wide in a fierce snarl. With terrifying speed, it lunged at Gajendra, closing its jaws with a sickening crunch around the elephant's hefty leg. The mighty elephant roared in agony as he felt the razor-sharp teeth sink into his flesh.

Gajendra thrashed his leg, twisted his body, and tried to pull free, but the crocodile's deadly grip only tightened. Desperately, he wrapped his trunk around a sturdy tree, hoping to anchor himself, but the crocodile's strength dragged him further into deeper waters. Gajendra, the strongest of all elephants, felt a growing sense of desperation. He used all his might and tried every trick he knew, but his energy waned with each effort. His cries echoed throughout the jungle, and his herd rushed to his aid. Friends and family tried to help, but the crocodile's grip was relentless. Despite the herd's strength on land, they were helpless in the water. They pulled and stretched, trying to free their leader, but the struggle proved futile. Eventually, their efforts slowed, and Gajendra was left alone.

Once the proud and mighty king of elephants, Gajendra now felt his strength ebbing away. The pull of the crocodile's jaws was unrelenting, and he knew he couldn't hold on much longer. As his body grew weaker and weaker, Gajendra's thoughts turned inwards. 'Is this the noose of destiny or the result of my ill fate? My strength, intelligence, and family couldn't save me from this crisis. I am helpless against it.'

In this moment of desperation, Gajendra cried out in prayer. He let go of all other support and, with a heart full of faith, began to call out from the depths of his being. With his trunk, he reached for a lotus floating on the river's surface and held it up toward the heavens in a plea for help. Hearing Gajendra's heartfelt prayer, God descended from the skies, filling the air with divine light. In one swift motion, God liberated Gajendra from the jaws of the crocodile, rescuing him from a grim fate. Having relinquished everything else, Gajendra found his solace and salvation in prayer.

'The Liberation of Gajendra' is a timeless Puranic story told by Shukdev to King Parikshit thousands of years ago.[*] Despite the passage of time, this simple yet profound tale continues to resonate with people because it touches upon universal themes. It underscores the power of faith and the transformative role of prayer, reminding us that in moments of crisis, spiritual connection can lead to liberation from worldly suffering.

This story, however, also sheds light on a deeper aspect of human nature. We often rely on intellect, skills, and inner strength to navigate life's challenges. To cope with

---

[*] 'The Elephant Gajendra's Crisis', *Bhaktivedanta Vedabase*, https://tinyurl. com/42p9fa2r (accessed 12 November 2024).

daily stresses, we turn to familiar comforts—our favourite shows, snacks, and cozy beds. We seek emotional support from friends and family. These habits act like a lifejacket, giving us a sense of security whether we are in shallow or turbulent waters. These comforting routines have become so ingrained that they shape our behaviour and even parts of our identity. It's as if the lifejacket has become a permanent part of our everyday attire.

However, when a tsunami strikes, when we're confronted with an overwhelming crisis, or when we face a desperate dilemma that seems unsolvable, our lifejackets may not be enough. It's in these moments, when all our skills, resources, and connections fall short, that we almost instinctively turn to faith. Whether it's a desperate cry for help, a hopeful whisper, or a call to a higher power, it's not uncommon for prayer to find its way to our lips. Amid profound uncertainty, we often seek comfort and guidance from something greater than ourselves.

Queen Kunti's prayer from the Mahabharat provides a profound example of how faith can shape our response to life's challenges. Throughout her life, Queen Kunti faced numerous trials and tribulations. She was exiled from her home, raised her five sons alone, and endured threats to her life and family. She survived a devastating war, witnessing the loss of many loved ones. During these turbulent times, prayer became her source of strength, enabling her to persevere despite overwhelming adversity.

When Queen Kunti's hardships ended, and she settled into a more comfortable life in a palace with her sons, she experienced a surprising shift in her spiritual journey. While enjoying the luxury and stability of her new life, she realized that she had begun to forget God. This self-awareness prompted her to re-evaluate her priorities and led her to express a unique and powerful prayer.

'My dear Krishna, Your Lordship has protected us from a poisoned cake, from a great fire, from cannibals, from the vicious assembly, from sufferings during our exile in the forest, and from the battle where great generals fought. And now you have saved us from the weapon of Asvatthama.

'I wish that all those calamities would happen again and again so that we could see you again and again, for seeing you means that we will no longer see repeated births and deaths.'*

Queen Kunti's outlook evolved, revealing an important truth about the nature of prayer. She recognized that the suffering she experienced in life had allowed her to strengthen her connection to the Divine. Through prayer, she found the resilience to overcome adversity, gaining inner strength and maturity. As her circumstances became more stable and comfortable, she noticed that without prayer, she was losing the chance to grow both personally and spiritually.

This realization led Queen Kunti to a powerful conclusion: she would even welcome turmoil again if it meant restoring her bond with God. She understood that prayer wasn't just a 'spare wheel' to use in times of crisis;

---

* 'Prayers by Queen Kuntī'. *The Hare Krishna Movement*, https://tinyurl.com/ycw6m5sj (accessed 11 November 2024).

it was a source of daily renewal and growth. Her shift in perspective can be a lesson for all of us—to consider how we use prayer and to recognize its broader impact on our lives. Rather than seeing prayer as a last resort, we can embrace it as a regular practice that sustains us, providing strength, clarity, and spiritual growth throughout our journey.

An inspiring story from France involves a war veteran who, despite losing a leg, entered a place of worship with hope and conviction. Upon seeing his injury, someone asked how this loss affected his faith. The veteran responded with striking confidence, stating that he didn't pray for his leg to grow back, but rather that his faith helped him find a meaningful life with his remaining leg. Through daily prayer, he gained the courage to move forward, the patience to endure, and the peace to accept what had happened.

Revered spiritual guru, Ramakrishna Paramahansa, once said, 'Just as we talk to each other, it's completely normal to share our happiness and sadness with God. Like a husband and wife who speak openly, we can have a conversation with God through prayer. It's good to take a moment each day to talk to God and express the feelings in our hearts. This regular practice will clear our minds and soften our speech. There's no doubt about it.'*

Mahant Swami Maharaj incorporates this style of prayer into many aspects of his day. He prays in traditional ways, through meditation and devotion, but also finds prayer in everyday activities such as eating, walking, or resting.

---

* Gharsabha Sahayika, Part 1 (Gujarati), pp. 194. Swaminarayan Aksharpith.

Through these routine activities, he mentally connects with the Divine, invoking a sacred presence. He converses with God like a close friend. When honoured or praised, he doesn't feel pride. Instead, he feels constantly blessed, thankful, and fulfilled. In quieter moments, Swamiji reflects on his gratitude for having found God and enjoys a contented existence free from expectations and desires.

Fascinatingly, Swamiji never prays for himself, preferring to focus on others. His mornings start by naming countries from around the world, expanding his compassion by praying for global peace, harmony, and prosperity. His nights are often filled with late prayers for the health and well-being of those who reach out to him. Through his approach, Mahant Swami Maharaj demonstrates that spirituality can be selfless and compassionate. He emphasizes that prayer isn't just a formal practice; it's a continuous and natural connection with the Divine, woven through our daily life.

Pramukh Swami Maharaj's words capture the essence of this practice: 'In prayer, it's not about the eloquence of your words, but the sincerity of your heart that counts. While some might see God as a spare wheel, true prayer is about recognizing that we need God in every moment. God is the source of all happiness, and troubles arise when we forget that.'

Prayer is not just a ritual for spiritual leaders—it's a profound aspect of daily life. It's a constant conversation with the Divine, a thread weaving through our existence. Through prayer, we can practice devotion, gratitude, compassion, peace, and harmony. It shapes us into better human beings, enriching our thoughts, actions, and relationships. Ultimately, prayer becomes a guiding light that illuminates the path to a more meaningful, fulfilling, and divine existence.

SEVA

What does it mean to be charitable? Is it a social responsibility, a quest for purpose, or a desire to bring a smile? Volunteering is undeniably important, but when it becomes seva, it transforms into something spiritual, selfless, and deeply meaningful. Seva is more than just the actions you take or the memories you create—it's about the way you treat people and who you become in the process.

From a distance, I could see red and white flags waving atop nine towering spires. I was visiting BAPS Swaminarayan Akshardham in New Jersey, often simply known as Akshardham. As I entered the campus, I faced the golden-hued murti of Bhagwan Swaminarayan standing in deep yogic meditation. His calm posture symbolizes focus, self-reflection, and peace. Moving forward, I saw families gathered and individuals meditating around a large stepped pond known as the Brahma Kunda. This stunning feature is a beautiful tribute to the planet's precious resources. As

I walked through the flowery, fragrant gardens towards the flags I had first seen, I was awestruck by the 213-foot-tall mandir. I studied the thousands of intricate stone carvings depicting deities, dancers, musicians, elephants, and scenes from nature. It stood as a vibrant expression of Indian culture, the largest of its kind in the Western world and the second largest globally. Everywhere I looked, there was something to inspire and enlighten me.

What struck me most amid the density of detail was that every inch was carved with a story—an untold story of what humanity can achieve when it unites in selfless service. A story that shows us that 'in the joy of others, lies our own'. A story of 12,500 volunteers. A story of 'seva'.

In Hinduism, 'seva' means selfless service. It represents the act of helping others, bringing them joy, and genuinely striving to make the world a better place. However, seva also benefits the person who serves—it is a spiritual practice that can transform one's life, giving it greater meaning and bringing us closer to God. Bhagwan Swaminarayan and his spiritual successors championed selfless service as a way of life deeply infused with spirituality. For the last two centuries, they have led by example, dedicating their lives to creating sacred spaces, pioneering charitable movements, serving the underprivileged, and empowering humanity.

Over the next few weeks, as I spent time at Akshardham, I learned the many stories behind its magnificent creation. One such story is that of 39-year-old Akash Patel from Charlotte, North Carolina. When he was just seven, his parents divorced, leaving his mother as the sole provider for him and his one-year-old brother. She worked two jobs to support her family. As Akash grew up, he witnessed his mother's struggle and worked hard to help her, eventually graduating and landing a successful career as a consultant for Ernst & Young.

With his progressing career, Akash saved enough to realize a meaningful dream. He bought a new car for his devoted mother and took over the payments on her house. He says it felt 'gratifying to give back to her after she had lovingly provided for me and my brother for so long'. Shortly after, Akash married, settled into a new home and welcomed a baby girl into his life. He found joy in having an idyllic suburban home with his family—'a place to call their own'. Akash felt immense happiness seeing his family content and loved. 'But more than that,' he reflects, 'I was glad that my daughter would never have to experience the kind of struggles that I went through.'

Despite his successful career, financial stability, and happy family, Akash still felt something was missing. He explained, 'My daughter was growing up fast, and we were thinking about the future. I had provided for her materially and was taking care of her physically, but what was I doing to teach her good values? Children learn best when we model good behaviour for them.' This realization was a turning point for Akash, who then decided to take two weeks off work in February 2022 to volunteer in the construction of Akshardham.

Akash was assigned to a team responsible for cutting and rigging stones. After a few days, he said, 'I realized I started feeling lighter. I was at ease. I began feeling peace, whereas before, I felt unsatisfied. The more I thought about it, the more I understood that my volunteer efforts were the cause of this new feeling.' For Akash, seva wasn't merely volunteering—it was an act of devotion. He noted:

> Every person I interacted with was engaged in devotion. This spiritual atmosphere prompted me to reflect on my own life. I was generating enough wealth to pay off my home in seven-and-a-half years; we had no immediate financial worries, and I was on a path where I could retire by the age of 50—yet I felt I wasn't doing enough. I realized that while money is crucial to support the people I love, beyond that, material wealth or possessions alone cannot provide purpose and meaning to us or our children.

After his two-week volunteering period, Akash drove to Boston to pick up his wife and daughter. He was taking them to see Akshardham while it was still under construction. During the car ride, he shared his experience of inner peace at Akshardham, and they talked about what they valued most in life. As they discussed, they both considered the possibility of moving to New Jersey for a couple of years. Akash could volunteer at Akshardham, while his wife continued working. However, they had concerns: Could they afford it? What would happen to the house they had just bought? How would it impact their daughter?

After a five-to-six-hour drive, they finally reached Robbinsville. As they walked to the 49-foot sacred murti of Bhagwan Swaminarayan in his yogic posture, the beauty of the sculpture reminded them of the many blessings they had received in life. At that moment, they made their decision: they would dedicate the next couple of years to selfless service at Akshardham. Akash recalls feeling 'an immense amount of joy'. Within 45 days, they wrapped up their lives in Charlotte and drove to New Jersey with their belongings in a trailer hitched to their SUV.

Reflecting after a year-and-a-half, Akash had a beaming smile on his face. He said, 'When we moved here, my daughter was a year old. She's learnt to walk, run, and talk while we've been here. My wife and I bring her to the mandir a few times a week before sunset. We love seeing her run around with a smile on her face. My wife and I spent many years generating wealth to provide our family with the material provisions we didn't have growing up. Now, when I'm volunteering at Akshardham, I'm amassing spiritual wealth in the form of contentment and inner peace. This is what I want to pass on to my daughter. We've gained beyond our hopes.'

Akash is continually reminded that the peace found within is worth more than any external achievement. Seva is not just about the actions we take or the good memories we create; seva is about who we become. Akash experienced this transformation first-hand. Another volunteer, Parth Desai, a student at Thomas Jefferson University, shared his own experiences of seva at Akshardham. He revealed, 'The atmosphere and love have helped me build confidence in myself. If there's one thing I've learnt about myself, it's that I'm more capable than I thought.'

When we work in teams—whether within a family or in a corporate environment—friction and tension often arise due to differing opinions and viewpoints. So how can we collaborate and work effectively? In seva opportunities, everyone aligns with one vision and intention: to serve selflessly. A volunteer explains, 'Seva has expanded the ways I can connect with others. Instead of getting frustrated when someone makes a mistake, I focus on what I can learn from them. I've become more honest with myself about what I should be doing better. The best way to improve myself, I think, is by seeing the good in everyone.' Guiding the Akshardham volunteers, Mahant Swami Maharaj highlighted an essential aspect of seva: 'I want everyone to serve with unity, mutual affection, and humility.'

Growing up performing seva at mandirs, BAPS volunteers are empowered to give selflessly to their communities. Dr Mayank Amin, a dedicated pharmacist in Pennsylvania, rallied local support and organized BAPS volunteers to vaccinate over 60,000 people.* During the Covid-19 pandemic, witnessing the vulnerability of many, he donned his Superman Halloween costume and jumped into action. He navigated through 14-inch snow to reach the distant homes of the elderly, disabled, and needy. His

---

* 'Getting Out of the Red with Mayank Amin'. *YouTube*, https://tinyurl.com/bdhd3hd5 (accessed 11 November 2024).

commitment to saving as many lives as possible often kept him up until 2 a.m.

Pointing to the big 'S' on the chest of his costume, Dr Amin explains, 'The "S" in Superman stands for "servant." Ever since I opened this pharmacy two years ago, it's always been my goal to serve the community. My guru, Pramukh Swami Maharaj, always taught us to go out into the world and help anyone, even if you don't know them.'[*]

Before opening a pharmacy, Dr Amin was in the events industry 'planning lavish weddings worth millions of dollars'. However, he shifted careers because he was only motivated by seva, not money. He explains, 'I didn't try to open a pharmacy to become a millionaire; I did it to make an impact on the community and show that when everyone comes together, amazing things happen.'[†]

Another medical practitioner, Dilip, also performed seva during the Covid-19 pandemic. When he heard about a government call for a medical volunteer, he drove 450 km to San Quentin Prison and booked a motel at his own cost. San Quentin, a maximum-security prison in California, houses some of the most dangerous and violent inmates in the United States. Despite the risks, Dilip compassionately served these inmates without judgement. Normally, he treats 15 to 20 patients daily, but due to the high demand, he attended to around 100 inmates each day.

---

[*] 'Good News: Superman Pharmacist Mayank Amin'. *YouTube*, https://tinyurl.com/mwjt35mk (accessed 11 November 2024).

[†] 'Good News: Superman Pharmacist Mayank Amin'. *YouTube*, https://tinyurl.com/3ux9dbc5 (accessed 11 November 2024).

The most challenging moment came when he was assigned to treat an inmate who had murdered a member of a family he personally knew and cared about. Even with the option to refuse, Dilip chose to treat him selflessly. 'My guru, Mahant Swami Maharaj, is my inspiration,' Dilip explains. 'He taught me that when you serve others, you must let go of the past and treat the human being in front of you. They are human like us, and they need help.'

Seva is about unconditional care: forgetting who we are, for the greater good of humankind. Great people come onto this earth to serve, and not to be served. A candle loses none of its light by lighting another candle. When performed with the right intention and guidance, seva transforms us into selfless, compassionate, and empowered human beings. Our life becomes a blessing. Serving others is a form of devotion to God and Guru, and this is one of the most valuable gifts of human life. With this awareness, we can recognize opportunities to serve within our families, friends, communities, and sacred spaces. If something truly matters to you, you'll make time for it.

A LOTUS IN THE DESERT

What are mandirs? Who do they belong to? What is their role? As the human race strides forward, the clamour for solutions for peace and fulfilment grows louder. And we find ourselves entering a new era, where sacred spaces like mandirs thrust themselves into renewed relevance. As we explore this context, we find ourselves in the shifting sands of the Middle East, where a Hindu swami and an Arab king forge an unexpected friendship, paving the way forward for global harmony.

Sharad is your typical 13-year-old boy, an enthusiastic cricketer on his school sports team, with a keen interest in Chemistry and Mathematics. Growing up in the United Arab Emirates, he engages daily with children from diverse backgrounds and cultures. As Diwali approaches, his curious school friends often inquire about his celebration of the festival. Slightly caught off guard by the question, Sharad shares everything he knows about his Indian heritage.

However, this discussion ignites a series of questions within his own mind.

Sharad sometimes travels to India during his vacations to reconnect with his grandparents. There, evenings become a time for the family to gather, with his grandparents often narrating the epic stories of Hinduism to impart Indian traditions and values. One of Sharad's cherished experiences during these visits is spending time at the temples. He explains, 'Mandirs are my favourite places to visit in India. It was where I felt most connected to my beliefs. I especially loved flying kites with my family at the mandir during the Uttarayan festival, and also admiring all the lights and decorations around the campus during Diwali.'

Despite being far from their homeland, Sharad's family had made every effort to keep him connected to his heritage. In the UAE, they join nearby families to celebrate major festivals, yet he never had the opportunity to fully immerse himself in his faith and culture. Children like Sharad may feel fortunate to have access to quality education for their personal and professional development, but they often struggle to establish a tangible connection to their heritage, culture, and identity.

Sharad's situation mirrors a common trend in our globalized world. While globalization offers opportunities for a multitude of advantages, maintaining connections to one's faith and cultural heritage can be challenging. In response, communities often establish sacred spaces in new locations, serving as bridges between past and present. Recognizing the importance of these places as symbols of community cohesion, the rulers of the United Arab Emirates (UAE) generously allocated land for the construction of a Hindu mandir for the Indian population.

Recently opened in 2024, the BAPS Hindu Mandir in the UAE is a captivating blend of beauty and spirituality. Situated in the desert dunes of Abu Dhabi, it resembles a majestic lotus blooming in an oasis of serenity. The mandir exudes an atmosphere of prayer, faith, and inspiration. At its core, the stone temple stands as a symbol of harmony, with seven spires that rise gracefully to honour the widely worshipped deities of Hinduism and the seven emirates of the UAE. In homage to the sacred rivers of India, the mandir's steps are graced by the flowing waters of the Ganga, Yamuna, and Saraswati, symbolizing purification and spiritual nourishment.

Every part of the BAPS Hindu Mandir encapsulates centuries of divinity within its stones, reflecting the rich heritage of Indian architecture and beauty. As visual beings, humans often use tangible objects such as paintings and sculptures to understand and convey ideas. Similarly, mandir architecture transcends cultural and linguistic barriers, offering a glimpse into the spiritual realm and inspiring us to seek beyond our mundane existence.

The stones adorning the BAPS Hindu Mandir in Abu Dhabi were all meticulously carved by skilled artisans in India, before being sent to Abu Dhabi to be assembled like a colossal jigsaw puzzle. Each spire of the mandir narrates the stories and teachings of the deities enshrined within, serving as a window into the timeless wisdom of Hinduism. Visitors are visually immersed in lessons of resilience, nobility, and loyalty as they explore the intricately carved depictions of Bhagwan Ram-Sita, the unity of the Pandav brothers from the Mahabharat, and fascinating depictions of the lives of Bhagwan Swaminarayan, Bhagwan Shiv-Parvati, Bhagwan Krishna, Bhagwan Jagannath, Bhagwan Tirupati Balaji, and Swami Shri Ayappa.

The Abu Dhabi Mandir also honours 15 ancient and modern civilizations in one embrace, encapsulating their wisdom and moral teachings within its stone carvings. From Egypt to Mesopotamia, China to Native America, Africa to Europe, and from India to the Middle East, the mandir's artwork transcends cultural boundaries. It invites people from diverse backgrounds to reflect on their journeys to seek greater understanding and enlightenment. These carvings serve not only to preserve ancient stories, but also to provide timeless guidance and inspiration for the present and future.

This diversity is not only evident in the mandir's artwork but also in its construction process. The land for the Hindu Mandir was generously provided by a Muslim ruler to a Hindu organization, while its lead architect hailed from the Christian faith. The foundational designer was a Buddhist, the contractor a Parsi, and the lead project director a Sikh. In 1997, Pramukh Swami Maharaj had envisioned a mandir in Abu Dhabi that would bring 'countries, cultures, and religions closer together' and today we see this as a reality.

While everyone learns and discovers themselves through the teachings of the mandir, its impact is perhaps most profound on children like Sharad. Serving as a bridge to his culture and a platform to celebrate his values, the Abu Dhabi Mandir has become a true home for him. The 'Brick by Brick' initiative enhanced a universal sense of belonging by encouraging visitors to sponsor and lay a brick in the construction process. At the forefront of this initiative were the mandir's young girls and boys, including Sharad. He reminisced, 'During the construction of the mandir, we children performed Hindu ceremonies for the bricks that formed its foundation. I led prayers for peace and harmony by reciting traditional Vedic Sanskrit verses. Witnessing the emotions and gratitude on the faces of visitors was truly memorable; tears often welled up in their eyes. Our enthusiasm for the completion of the mandir was shared with all communities. Guiding the guests made me realize the broader significance of the mandir. For me, it was not only a place to call home and learn about my heritage, but also a beacon of peace and harmony to share with the world.'

Prapti was among the young girls who participated in the 'tiny treasures' project, where 100 children painted inspirational messages onto beautiful marble stones, which were then gifted to visitors. One day, a volunteer noticed Prapti painting alone while her friends were playing together. Intrigued, the volunteer asked her why she was still painting instead of joining her friends. With a smile, Prapti responded, 'This is my mandir! How can I not finish this task!'

The children also guide guests through the mandir complex, narrating the stories and universal values they represent. 'We recently welcomed diplomats and ambassadors from over 42 nations in the traditional Hindu manner,' Sharad reminisced, 'and shared our contributions.' Upon receiving the tiny treasures as a gift, one ambassador read the message aloud, 'We Love, We Serve.' She then expressed her thoughts and gratitude, 'I see this profound message alive in all the boys and girls here today. I will always keep this by my bedside as a reminder every morning to live with this purpose.'

The same boy, who once struggled to connect with his heritage, now confidently expresses his cultural identity to his schoolmates. 'Before I got involved in the mandir, I was very shy,' Sharad explains. 'But now I feel confident and enjoy working in teams. During our Wednesday school assemblies, I was asked to present Hinduism to the entire school, grades 1 to 12. Before, I would have declined to speak, but because of the mandir, I proudly shared my traditions, culture, and beliefs. My teachers and friends were super impressed!'

'Through volunteering and weekly classes, I've witnessed the children's growth,' Pranit Dhakaan, a young mandir volunteer, explained. 'Before the mandir, they were unsure of their identity. But now, they confidently share the universal messages of Hinduism with their friends. They've become more connected, caring, and generous. Not only have they developed personally, academically, and spiritually, but I've seen them transform into global ambassadors of peace and harmony.'

Mandirs such as the BAPS Hindu Mandir in Abu Dhabi exemplify a dedication to preparing the next generation, equipping them to lead lives of purpose and significance. By connecting them to their personal faith and encouraging them to serve broader communities, these mandirs play a crucial role in shaping the future. With the backing of 20,000 BAPS Youth Engagement volunteers, 150,000 girls and boys, like Prapti and Sharad, are empowered in mandirs spanning 40 countries.* They find avenues to connect with their heritage, enrich their lives, and make meaningful contributions to the world.

Four years before the completion of the Abu Dhabi mandir, Mahant Swami Maharaj envisioned its purpose. 'A new era will dawn.' he declared, 'Each and every piece of land will be filled with miracles—miracles of positive transformations. The mandir will serve as a haven of unity, support, culture, and civilization.' With over two million visitors passing through its gates in the first year since opening to the public, the vision is becoming a reality. The generosity of the UAE rulers and the foresight of Mahant Swami Maharaj have paved the way for both harmony and transformation. Witnessing the empowered children of Abu Dhabi fills me with hope for future generations.

---

* 'Children's Day: Celebrating the Future', *PSM100*, https://tinyurl.com/ y674dr36 (accessed 11 November 2024).

THE ROLE OF GURUS

The brushstrokes of those around us paint our canvas. From the clothes we wear to the language we use and even our career paths, our lives are influenced by countless people. Superstars, fashion icons, and innovators set trends, while family, friends, and teachers shape our views and life decisions. We crave inspiration, but rather than simply being led, let's take a proactive approach. Why not seek out role models who will empower us to become the best versions of ourselves?

Standing at the edge of the pool, I could hear the noise of my classmates urging me to take the plunge. Some had already dived in, but fear gripped me tightly. I had never been able to swim properly, yet I had committed to these classes. I knew I had to overcome my apprehensions and give it a try. But before I could gather my courage, a sudden nudge from behind sent me tumbling into the coldness. Panic seized me as the water filled my nose and mouth. I gasped for air and cried out for help. But to my dismay, no one seemed to notice my distress.

Thrashing about wildly, I fought desperately against the water. I started kicking my legs with all my might, and gradually, with each powerful kick, I drew closer to the edge. Finally, my coach's outstretched hand pulled me to safety. Collapsing on the poolside, exhausted and relieved, I couldn't help but express my frustration to the coach about his delayed intervention. His response, however, inspired a newfound understanding: 'I was always here, watching, ready to jump in at any time. But by allowing you to struggle, you discovered your strength and learned to swim.'

Whether serving as coaches, teachers, or guides, these individuals typically possess expertise or skill. We entrust them because they can help us realize our potential. We are bound by what we think we can do, but a wise mentor discerns our true capabilities. They recognize our innate potential and motivate us to surpass perceived boundaries, enabling us to achieve greater heights. This principle holds true in both our worldly and spiritual spheres. When my friend, Haresh Moradiya, recounted the swimming experience to Pramukh Swami Maharaj, I stood beside him, carefully awaiting Swamiji's response. Swamiji's words were so profound that they became the turning point in my life.

But first, let's delve into the concept of a 'guru'. While we often encounter the term used in various contexts, what is its original meaning? Dating back to ancient times, the term 'guru' refers to a spiritual teacher, mentor, or master—someone capable of guiding others to awaken their true eternal self, known as the 'atma'. In its essence, 'gu' represents 'darkness', and 'ru' signifies 'to remove'. Therefore, the guru is the one who dispels the darkness of ignorance, leading us into the light of truth. Their profound wisdom not only eradicates our biases and complexes, but also broadens our narrow perception of both our existence and the world we inhabit. As Krishna Bhagwan states in the Bhagavad Gita, 'Learn the truth by approaching the spiritual guru [. . .] Such an enlightened individual can impart knowledge to you because they have seen the truth.'*

The Vedic texts emphasize the indispensable role of a guru on the spiritual journey. In particular, the Mundaka Upanishad elaborates on the essential qualities that define the ultimate guru, employing three key terms: 'shrotriyam', 'Brahma', and 'nishtha'.† Firstly, 'shrotriyam' characterizes the guru as one who not only comprehends the essence of the Vedic texts, but also embodies profound understanding, living that wisdom in every aspect of life. Secondly, 'Brahma' signifies the spiritual authority of the guru. In the BAPS tradition, 'Brahma' is synonymous with 'Akshar' or 'Aksharbrahma'—an enlightened being devoid of worldly desires and pure of heart. Lastly, the guru should epitomize 'nishtha', embodying unshakeable conviction and unwavering steadfastness in God. By possessing such qualities, the guru is deemed ideally equipped to guide others towards spiritual excellence.

---

* Bhagavad Gita 4.34
† Mundaka Upanisad 1.2.12

The principle of the guru-disciple succession (*parampara* system) is not limited to Vedic texts, but is also found in many global cultures and traditions. In India, several successions of guru-disciple traditions are said to have started from the dawn of civilization. Others began with the early appearances of particular incarnations or when the teachings of a particular sage gave them prominence. Each guru in a succession is responsible for preserving and disseminating their tradition's teachings. By committing oneself to an authentic guru with an unbroken lineage, one gains access to the original revelation.

What would we do if we wanted to reach a ripe mango at the top of a mango tree? Several people climb the tree and form a line. The person at the top hands down the mango to the person below, who passes it down to the next, until the mango reaches you on the ground unbruised. The guru connects us to the current of truth, while the community of aspirants confirms that truth by living its spirit. The guru becomes necessary when spiritual knowledge is not immediately perceptible to us. Furthermore, in the practical application of spiritual knowledge, we will encounter many doubts and difficulties. To resolve this, the guru plays an essential role.

Nevertheless, there is a difference between a material and a spiritual teacher. This should be understood clearly. While material teachers require only theoretical knowledge about a subject, a spiritual teacher not only pursues theoretical knowledge, but also has practical realization too. During a trip to India, the renowned English writer Somerset

Maugham encountered the esteemed sage Ramana Maharshi, an encounter he found profoundly enlightening. Reflecting on his experience, he wrote, 'It is a mistake to think that those holy men of India lead useless lives. They are a shining light in the darkness. [. . .] When a man becomes pure and perfect, the influence of his character spreads so that those who seek truth are naturally drawn to him.'[*]

To encounter such an enlightened guru is perhaps the greatest spiritual blessing one can receive. In the BAPS Swaminarayan tradition, the divinity of Bhagwan Swaminarayan continues through the living, breathing spiritual guru, who guides, blesses, and inspires spiritual seekers in their quest for truth, as well as serving humanity as a whole. For more than seven decades, Pramukh Swami Maharaj perceptively gauged the pulse of society, addressing people's concerns and offering practical solutions. This ability stemmed from his extensive experience of personally interacting with and counselling millions of individuals from diverse backgrounds and ages. Fascinatingly, his personality remained accessible to both world leaders and tribal villagers alike. His genuine care reached four generations. Selflessly dedicated to the moral and spiritual upliftment of others, Pramukh Swami Maharaj devoted his life to this noble cause. His teachings transcended self-interest or bias, and his words were both profound and practical.

---

[*] Maugham, W. S., 1944, The Razor's Edge—Chapter Six. https://tinyurl.com/yeue655r (accessed 11 November 2024).

Today, Mahant Swami Maharaj—the current guru of BAPS—remains accessible through spiritual travels, cultural events, correspondence, and phone calls. During these encounters, many experience peace, joy, and renewed purpose. He inspires values of personal faith, virtuous living, selfless service, and global harmony. Mahant Swami Maharaj's guidance continues to inspire me profoundly. My gurus have shaped who I am today by unlocking my latent potential. Every time I speak, I honour my gurus, as everything I may have achieved stems from their inspiration and guidance.

I found that taking the guidance of a true guru is the easiest, shortest, and surest path to attaining not only the highest truth but also peace and happiness. The guru guides, encourages, and blesses a genuine student to attain spiritual perfection. The right guidance from the right person at the right time can be transformative. This is the most impactful lesson I have discovered in life.

So back to the swimming incident. It was in the late 1980s during my college years in Vallabh Vidyanagar, that this memorable encounter unfolded. Seated amidst a group of eager youths, I found myself in the presence of Pramukh Swami Maharaj. His demeanour was both majestic yet light-hearted as he occupied a chair. We eagerly gathered around him, sitting cross-legged on the floor. As we narrated the story of our swimming coach, he took an opportunity to teach us a profound lesson: 'On the spiritual path, we all require a guru like a lifeguard, who can guide us across the vast ocean of existence. Firstly, you must develop faith in the guru's expertise. Then cultivate a thirst for learning, like you did for swimming. Most importantly, when a true guru expands your horizons beyond that which you perceive and know, be ready to persevere and trust in their wisdom.'

More than 30 years have passed, yet this memory remains as vivid as if it happened yesterday: Swamiji's expressive face, his gentle voice, and, most importantly, the profound impact of his words. They etched a crucial life lesson into my being. Since then, I have swum further than I could have imagined and discovered strength I never knew existed. Even now, as I confront uncharted waters ahead, I am filled with a deep sense of assurance, knowing my gurus are watching over me, guiding me, and always ready to lend a helping hand.